The Language of Female Leadership

Also by Judith Baxter
POSITIONING GENDER IN DISCOURSE: A Feminist Methodology

Also Edited by Judith Baxter
SPEAKING OUT: The Female Voice in Public Contexts

The Language of Female Leadership

Judith Baxter
Senior Lecturer in Applied Linguistics, Aston University, UK

First published 2010 by
PALGRAVE MACMILLAN

Palgrave Macmillan in the UK is an imprint of Macmillan Publishers Limited, registered in England, company number 785998, of Houndmills, Basingstoke, Hampshire RG21 6XS.

Palgrave Macmillan in the US is a division of St Martin's Press LLC, 175 Fifth Avenue, New York, NY 10010.

Palgrave Macmillan is the global academic imprint of the above companies and has companies and representatives throughout the world.

Palgrave® and Macmillan® are registered trademarks in the United States, the United Kingdom, Europe and other countries.

ISBN-13: 978-1-4039-9788-3   hardback

This book is printed on paper suitable for recycling and made from fully managed and sustained forest sources. Logging, pulping and manufacturing processes are expected to conform to the environmental regulations of the country of origin.

A catalogue record for this book is available from the British Library.

A catalogue record for this book is available from the Library of Congress.

Printed and bound in Great Britain by
CPI Antony Rowe, Chippenham and Eastbourne

Contents

List of Figures

Acknowledgements

I am deeply grateful to my husband, Brian, for patiently reading drafts of this book, often several times, and providing me with encouragement, support, constructive criticism and advice. Without his inspiration, this book would not have been achieved.

My thanks also go to all the senior people who supported or took part in the research studies discussed in this book. Special thanks in particular go to: Nancy Badoo, Mike Caldwell, Peter Erskine, Martyn Lambert, Sandra McCleod, Rhodora Palomar, Tessa Raeburn, Steve Robertson, Ian Ryder, Dave Smith, Meryl Strang, Jonathan Turpin and Gemma Webb.

Map of the Book

The broad purpose of this book is to ask whether *language* is a reason why women are under-represented at senior level in the business world. Within that broad purpose, the book has two principal aims. The *first* is to assess whether there is indeed a language of female leadership, and the *second* is to ask how female leaders can utilise language as effectively as possible to achieve their business goals. This book therefore puts forward a case for the significance of language to female leadership, and to achieve this, is organised in eight chapters. Chapter 1 sets the scene for the rest of the book looking at the economic, cultural and linguistic background to the case, and introducing key terms and constructs. At the centre of the book is the notion that the language of female leadership takes place in three types of corporation: Male-Dominated; Gender-Divided or Gender-Multiple.

In Chapter 2, I show how the language and gender theory of *dominance* (Fishman 1978; Pauwels 1989; Spender 1980) is well placed to explain the discourse features of Male-Dominated corporations. Gender dominance as a theory emerged in the 1970s when feminist linguistics was in its infancy yet second-wave feminism (Baxter 2003; Mills 2003) was at its height. While times have moved on, certain features of the Male-Dominated corporation still prevail within some businesses today, often in the form of gendered discourses. Chapter 2 describes the Male-Dominated corporation in more detail, and its use of gender-neutral strategies to disguise and yet to perpetuate its outdated cultural stance on gender. Such 'gender-neutral' strategies include the endorsement of a range of stereotypical role models for female leaders, masculinised metaphors in corporate language; and a lack of contestation of hegemonic gendered discourses.

In Chapter 3, I explore how the influential language and gender theory of *difference* (Coates 2004; Tannen 1990; Holmes 2001) is well placed to conceptualise practices in Gender-Divided corporations. As a possible consequence of second wave feminist activism, there was a reassessment in the 1980s and 1990s of the qualities and attributes associated with women (Mills 2003). These were no longer perceived as weaknesses but as possible strengths that could benefit the productivity of businesses and professions. This chapter explores the language and gender 'difference' theory (e.g. Coates 2004; Holmes 2001; Tannen 1994), and shows how this theory was taken up and applied by organisation studies (Helgesen 1990; Rosener 1990), and used both by networks of female leaders and by business leaders and pundits to redefine the identity of leadership, even distinguishing it conceptually from management (Kotter 2001).

In Chapter 4, I discuss how *discourse* theory (also known as the 'social constructionist' approach; Butler 1990; Crawford 1995; Cameron 1997) is very well placed to explain the construct of a Gender-Multiple corporation, which considers language as social practice and therefore constitutive of all human activity. In the post-feminist times of the early 21st century, people have been less concerned to define themselves primarily by their sex or gender, and more interested in recognising that people have multiple identities with experience and expertise in widely varying areas of their lives. At the same time, gender is regarded as an important distinguishing feature, but not one that should cause undue prejudice or harm to a person's domestic life or professional career. This approach helps to explain the notion of multiplicity, while recognising the continuing prevalence of gendered discourses that can both enable and damage people (Sunderland 2004). Chapter 4 explores the discourse approach and its implications for leadership under three headings: discourses in the organisation, the social construction of gender identities, and Communities of Practice (CoPs). These first two aspects of discourse theory inevitably overlap in that institutional discourses work to construct gender identities, while identities act upon discourses in order to shape and change them, so the three sections will be reflexive about this interrelationship. With its postmodernist roots, discourse theory has critiqued both the gender dominance and gender difference theories (Butler 1990; Cameron 2003; Crawford 1995), but also recognises the value of their application to particular cultural contexts at particular times. Arguably, such theoretical paradigms continue to add some value to other parts of the world where corporations are characterised much more explicitly by male-dominated or gender-divided practices (e.g. De Kadt 2002).

In Chapter 5, I present a case study from an ongoing research project (Baxter 2008), of how the language of female leadership adapts to and constructs best practice in different types of gendered corporations. I investigate some of the linguistic strategies female leaders have evolved to survive in male-dominated settings, and to thrive in gender-multiple contexts. The research study I use here reveals how senior women routinely experience negative evaluations of their work. As a response, they have developed a special kind of linguistic expertise in order to be viewed positively as effective leaders. Women leaders have to be more concerned with the *impact* of their language upon their professional colleagues than male leaders have to be, and consequently have developed a range of linguistic strategies to counter negative judgements.

In Chapter 6, I discuss a second case study from my ongoing research project (Baxter 2008) of one multi-national corporation, which might be described as 'gender-multiple'. I examine the case of a female managing director who, while not flawless, has developed a sophisticated range of linguistic strategies in order to exercise her authority and fulfil business goals in effective and successful ways. The chapter conducts a micro-analysis of the 'speech acts' (Austin 1962; Searle 1969) used by this female leader to chair and run a management meeting productively. It also conducts a macro-analysis of the gendered discourses shaping these meetings and how such discourses are drawn upon or contested in order to get business done successfully.

In Chapter 7, I propose an aspiration for female leadership by reviewing how the Gender-Multiple corporation can be best 'talked into being': a responsibility that is in the interests of all senior people. Based on good practice, I present a range of strategies for the individual leader (such as the negotiated use of humour, politeness and authority) and strategies for the corporation (such as appointing 'linguistic champions'; ways of contesting gendered discourses).

Finally in Chapter 8, I give my response to the driving question of this book, 'Is language a reason why female leaders continue to be under-represented at senior level?' I also draw some conclusions about whether or not there is a distinctive language of female leadership.

1
Leading Talk

Introduction

This scene takes place in a boardroom of a large multi-national company in the centre of London, UK:

Jan: no no (.) we're not talking about that (.) we're talking about the communication and the interaction between the people around this table and the Irish business and the people in the Irish business

Tim: well yep

Jan: yes? so that you need to come back and say exactly what you feel is best so we actually sit down and discuss it?

Tim: yep fair point

Jan: OK then alright so shall we have a break for five minutes is that a good idea? it's like pulling teeth (*laughs*) it's supposed to be the easy part of it (.) it's supposed to be the nice part of it (*no reactions from rest of team*).

(See Appendix 1 for transcription conventions.)

In this short extract, Jan, the Managing Director of the company's UK Division, reaches the end of a long discussion with her mainly male management team in which they have been arguing over the need to improve communication in the business. By this point in the meeting, Jan looks exhausted and has to go outside for a much-needed cigarette. She looks visibly shaken by the experience. Her colleagues avoid her during the meeting break. An hour before, she opened the discussion by saying:

> **Jan:** the change management in the business has been <u>shite</u>
> so that's why I've put it on the agenda to decide what
> we're going to communicate (.) how we're going to com-
> municate and who's going to do it (3) so I want us to be
> specific

'Communication in the business' is clearly an important agenda item meriting a full and exploratory discussion among the team. But could the meeting have gone better? During the meeting, Jan was not overly heavy-handed and consulted team members at every stage. From the limited evidence of this extract, the male members of her team were not being deliberately difficult: Tim accepts his boss's point of view. So, was it the judgemental way in which Jan opened this agenda item that caused the protracted discussions among her team? Could she have presented and sought the opinions of her team in a more inclusive way? How should senior women use leader-ship language? Is there any difference in the way they should go about it compared to their male colleagues?

You are unlikely to find answers to these questions in the hundreds of business and management books published on leadership each month, or even within the increasing number specialising in female leadership (e.g. Eagly and Carli 2007; Hayward 2005; Vinnicombe *et al* 2009). A central issue explored in many of these female leadership books is the 'glass ceiling': women are still missing from the top of business corporations, which has implications for women at every level. Many of these books on women's leadership examine the bar-riers blocking women's career paths to leadership and consider what can be done to ensure a faster pace of changes so that more women's talents are utilised by their organisations to their mutual benefit. The focus is upon the economic, socio-cultural and political reasons for the challenges that face senior women, such as a lack of female role models, insufficient mentoring or networks for women, an inflexible working day, the work-life (im)balance, organisational politics, poor impression management, and so on (Singh 2008). A commercial by-product of such literature is the burgeoning body of self-help guides offering 'roadmaps' for career women to help them improve their chances of being appointed to boards and once there, establish their authority with their (often) male colleagues (e.g. Thomson and Graham 2008).

Unfortunately – and crucially – what is missing in these discussions about women and leadership is the insight that *language* may be a very powerful reason why women are under-represented at leadership level and find the going tough at the top. The way women talk and interact with their colleagues at different levels, and the way they are talked about, can offer valuable insights into their continuing minority status at senior level. This is despite a purported female superiority in language acquisition and verbal abilities (e.g. Kimura 1999; Pinker 2008), and a cultural perception that women are generally more eloquent, socially skilled and responsive speakers. So this is *not* about some sort of female linguistic deficiency – quite the opposite! Senior women are often highly skilled and astute communicators with a sophisticated awareness of the effect of their words on others. The business world is a context in which women can also demonstrate their abilities, strengths, sense of vision and energy, and much of this can be effectively achieved through language. The way we speak – our speaker identities – has a key place in determining just how successful individual women and men will be as managers and as leaders. It is often women rather than men who realise this. What both women and men leaders need, however, is greater *linguistic awareness* of how they and others use language and the profound effects this has on colleagues. In the short term, women need to become both linguistically aware and *expert* if they are to survive and to thrive in their organisations. Given that there are still many barriers blocking women's career paths to leadership positions (Sealy, Vinnicombe and Singh 2008), linguistic astuteness and expertise could be a crucial means of accelerating culture change to allow for a genuinely more diverse and women-friendly business world.

This book is about the extraordinary role of *language* in enabling women, primarily, to be effective and powerful leaders in the business world. It will show how the language we use in our everyday interactions with colleagues is fundamental to *constructing* effective leadership identities, roles, relationships, practices and even corporate cultures. Language is therefore so much more than just communication.

So the broad purpose of this book is to explore the role of language in female leadership, and to ask whether *language* is a reason why business women are under-represented at senior level. Within that broad purpose, the book has two aims. The first is to explore whether there *is* in fact a language of leadership that is exclusive to women. If the answer is 'yes', is there simply one definitive language with specific features and characteristics? Or are there a variety of versions depending on the business context or the corporate culture? If the answer is 'no', then the question to ask is 'do female leaders really speak exactly like men?' Indeed, is it really possible to generalise in this way? The *second* aim is to explore ways that female leaders can utilise language as effectively as possible to achieve their business goals, and in certain contexts, to counter negative evaluations made against them *because they are women,* which may ultimately hamper their career progress.

To achieve these aims, the book will explore the following six aspects of 'leadership language':

- The power of language in shaping leadership identities, roles, and relationships at work as well as in contributing to getting work done effectively
- The possible role of language as a factor in explaining the under-representation of female leaders at board level
- Features that characterise the language of effective leadership for both females and males
- Any features that seem to typify the female language style
- How some work settings create a negative linguistic environment for female leaders, in terms of the way these represent and stereotype women
- Ways of creating a *productive* linguistic environment for women leaders, in which female talents can grow and flourish, and in which women can be regarded as influential role models for junior colleagues. This may also allow women's realities to emerge in the corporate world so that they can influence and inform top-level decisions being made.

To understand why senior women have a tougher job in the workplace than men, the rest of the chapter will provide a brief economic, linguistic and cultural background to the subject of the language of female leadership, and consider the relevance of gender to work settings.

The economic background

> Thirty years on from the Sex Discrimination Act, women rightly expect to share power. But as our survey shows, that's not the reality...in business, no one can afford to fish in half the talent pool in today's competitive world.
>
> (Watson, Equal Opportunities Commission 2007)

The way female leaders use language is constantly affected by the specific business contexts in which they work, which are shaped in turn by broader economic and political conditions. Today, there are stark, and arguably, shocking differences between the distribution of males and females at senior leadership level in multi-national companies based in the UK and elsewhere. Despite almost 30 years of equal opportunities and educational reforms in the western world, and increasing numbers of women in management, there is still a tiny minority of women in senior leadership positions. Around the world in most developed nations, women are missing from the top of corporations, despite the business case for gender diversity in decision-making, the fact that women make major purchasing decisions as consumers, and most surprisingly, that 68 women have led their countries as presidents and prime ministers, and 11 countries have selected at least two women as presidents or prime ministers (EOC 2007). Men continue to occupy the most powerful roles in most multi-national companies, not just in Britain but worldwide, whereas women are still a rare presence in boardrooms. A survey conducted by *The Business* Magazine (Heath, Steiner, Cave and Boyle 2007) states that 94% of 'public limited companies' (plc) directors are still men. This has barely changed over the past decade with the share of female directors increasing from 4.6% in 1997 to 6.1% at the start of 2007. Even younger directors, according to the survey, are predominantly male: of the 930 respondents aged between 30 and 39, only 10.3% were female. An improvement did occur in 2008 when the percentage of female plc board directors moved up to 11% (Sealy, Vinnicombe and Singh 2008) but it remains to be seen whether this is sustained in future years. The *Business*

Magazine implies that female under-representation is a waste of a potential talent pool:

> At a time when women are continuing to make gains in most fields of life – girls out-shine boys at A-levels, make up 48% of the intake at Oxford and have made great strides in all professions – they remain a tiny minority in senior business positions.
>
> (Heath, Steiner, Cave and Boyle 2007: 22)

In addition, the Equal Opportunities Commission (EOC 2007) in Britain calculated that at the current rate it will take another 20 years to achieve equality between males and females in Civil Service top management, 40 years to achieve an equal number of senior women in the judiciary, 60 years to gain equality of female directors in FTSE 100 companies, and 100 years to achieve an equal number of women in the Houses of Parliament.

From a linguistic perspective, if women leaders are being excluded from boardrooms, they are also being excluded from having a voice at the board table. Women are not contributing to the executive communities that determine business policies and practices. This exclusion of 'the female voice' is a serious matter within the business community because there are tangible and measurable consequences. As 'glass ceiling' literature has argued (e.g. Eagly and Carli 2007; Hayward 2005; Vinnicombe *et al* 2009), the exclusion of women leads to a loss of productivity and performance in the organisation, and women as employees continue to earn significantly less than their male counterparts. Indeed, the 'glass ceiling' continues to operate in professions where women are not necessarily out-numbered by men, and where public rhetoric is explicitly supportive of equal opportunities, such as academia. Riley, Frith, Archer and Veseley (2006) reported that female professors still form a tiny minority of the overall cohort, and women's jobs tend to be more casualised and junior than those of their male counterparts.

Clearly, there are complex economic, cultural and material reasons why the glass ceiling persists, as testified by the considerable literature on organisations (see Halford and Leonard 2001, for a summary). However, McConnell-Ginet (2000) has argued that raising *linguistic awareness* is as essential as legal or political action towards sustainable social change: businesses need to know about the impact of language to make changes to the gender balance in the boardroom. In order to understand this linguistic impact as a factor in the under-representation of female leaders, I want to describe the changing ways in which language has been conceptualised by research, so that today it is seen as 'much more than just communication'.

The significance of language

> The alternative to seeing language as describing an independent reality is to recognise the power of language that allows us to freshly interpret our experience – and might enable us to bring forth new realities.
>
> (Senge 1994: 27)

Quite recently I was observing a senior management meeting as part of this research, and was chatting to the marketing director during the coffee break. He asked me why on earth I was interested in the language he and his colleagues were using at the meeting. 'After all', he said, 'language is just the *outcome* of what people think; it isn't an important part of leadership at all.' Why wasn't I looking at more substantive issues of leadership like the topics of discussion, the problems being solved, the decisions being made? This wasn't the moment to peddle my argument that language is not some kind of a by-product, but an essential means of enacting leadership effec-tively, and that topics of discussion, decisions and problems are always constructed and even transformed through language. I might have simply confirmed a popular stereotype of academics that their heads are in the clouds and their feet have left the ground!

But in fact this manager was expressing an equally commonly held view that words are simply 'containers of meaning', and that language has a simple, mechanistic function of transmitting a message between a speaker and a listener. Early models viewed communication as the process by which an 'encoder' sends a message to a 'receiver' by means of a 'channel' (such as speech and/or a telephone). Communication was judged successful if there was an absence of 'noise' or disturb-ance, as illustrated by the well-known Shannon and Weaver (1949) model.

In short, this model (see Figure 1.1) conceptualises commun-ication as a *process*, a simple transmission of information from

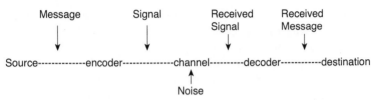

Figure 1.1   Shannon and Weaver's communication model (1949)

A to B, a matter of input-output. This basic, linear, mechanistic approach was then reflected in old-style manuals on communication skills which held the instrumental view that:

> Communication in business is an exchange of ideas, messages and concepts relating to the achievement of commercial objectives.
>
> (Katz 1989: 4)

So according to this model, communication would be deemed effective if, for example, the listener had understood an instruction given by the speaker and subsequently carried it out correctly. The problem with this model is that it doesn't recognise the role of multi-dimensional psychological, cultural and contextual factors in terms of how we communicate, except as an unwelcome disturbance to the purity of the communication flow.

By the 1980s, such 'process' models were being challenged by new models of communication that borrowed insights from anthropology, sociolinguistics, marketing, organisational studies and management (e.g. Bargiela-Chiappini and Harris 1997; Holmes 2000; McCall and Cousins 1990). According to these new 'context' models, language is viewed more holistically as responsive to and simultaneously shaping contexts or 'communities of practice' (Lave and Wenger 1991). In simpler terms, people's speech doesn't happen in a vacuum: it is constantly adapting to the *context:* who you are speaking to, what the purpose and topic of the conversation is, and in which setting the conversation is taking place, as shown in Figure 1.2.

So, this more fluid, dynamic model suggests that communication varies contextually according to the particular 'community of practice' (CofP). That is, this dynamic model involves the changing identity and relationships of the participants, the purpose or goals of their encounter, the setting in which they gather, and the various

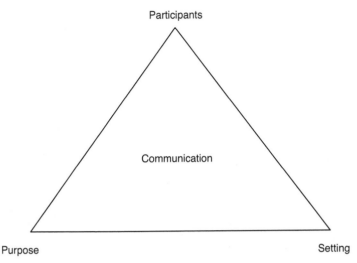

Figure 1.2 The dynamic or contextual model, adapted from Holmes 2001

topics of their discussion. This approach views communication as altogether less predictable, more socially variable and more context-dependent than the process model. But the problem with this model is that there is still a sense in which language remains 'a container of meaning' which simply shifts shape according to changing contextual factors.

More recently, a *discourse* (also known as 'social constructionist') approach to language has strongly influenced models of communication. This approach considers that language is a key form of *social practice* (Butler 1990; Cameron 2001; Crawford 1995; Foucault 1980). What this means is that language doesn't simply contain or reflect meaning, but actively *constructs* and *performs* it to provide our sense of social reality. So, individuals use language as a vital *resource* to present themselves in different ways and thereby to construct multiple identities for themselves as required by role, position, relationship and context. The discourse approach views language as *constitutive* of individual identities in two senses: it offers a set of resources by which people have the 'agency' or authority to perform leadership, but it also features within broader institutional practices or *discourses* (Foucault 1980), a point I return to in Chapter 4. These 'discourses' are sets of assumptions, beliefs, ways of thinking, speaking, talking and writing about others that come to be dominant and therefore to be 'common sense' within an organisation (Baxter 2003; Brewis 2001). They are key forms of social practice – or structuring forces within individual behaviour – that are predominantly enacted through language. They encourage approved or established ways of thinking, talking and representing others in the world, which in this case may include our sense of being male or female. Using leadership as an example, discourses may serve to endorse a female leader's sense of authority, but they may also serve to constrain or undermine it.

The discourse approach to language is by far the most valuable model of the three above for understanding the language of female leadership. This is because it provides insights into the complex and fluid ways in which senior women are positioned within corporate life. It also offers a means of analysing language use on both an individual and an institutional level. On an individual level, senior women have some 'agency' in that they have access to a language of authority for use with subordinates, but they are also constrained by the competitive linguistic authority of their peers and more senior colleagues. On an institutional level, senior women can be supported but also constrained by institutional discourses that reward 'appropriate' speech and behaviour, and penalise 'inappropriate' speech and behaviour (Brewis 2001; Foucault 1980). Discourse theory provides a means of analysing the complex interactions between individual agency and institutional level discourse, and how this often positions female leaders in competing and conflicting ways.

In sum, a discourse approach involves the dynamic interaction of three key elements: individual agency, discourses and linguistic interaction, as shown in Figure 1.3.

The discourse approach is also closely associated with a social semiotic understanding of how language works (e.g. Kress and Leeuwen 1996), which regards all modes of language such as dress, appearance, body language, office design, possessions, choice of car, as conveying culturally-specific meanings. As a linguist, I will be primarily concerned with the *verbal* mode – the words people speak and write. But of course verbal communication has a close relationship with *non*-verbal communication (NVC). Body language such as the use of gestures, eye contact and body posture brings our speech alive and gives

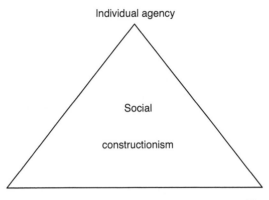

Figure 1.3 The discourse model of language

expression to our words. NVC continues to play a major role in the training and development of communication skills, as a tool to achieve effective leadership. Within a discourse view of language, NVC is more than simply a tool: it is an index of our identities, roles and relationships, and the way we manage these through interactions. It will be important to consider the role of NVC later in asking whether or not there is a distinctive language of female leadership.

I shall now review the *relationship* between leadership and language to give you an idea of how it has been previously conceptualised within research literature. I then propose an alternative approach which places the main focus of interest on how leadership is enacted through language.

Leadership and language

Leadership is a complex concept which has been studied from myriad perspectives both in organisational studies and across diverse disciplines (see Grint 1997 for overview). A strong theme across disciplines is to gain a better understanding of what constitutes 'effective' leadership and which factors have an influence on leadership performance (Singh 2008). Early assumptions that leaders were born rather than made were subsequently replaced by theories which focused on traits or behaviours displayed by 'effective' leaders.

One influential body of work within the specialist sub-field of women's leadership is that produced by Cranfield University's Centre for Women Business Leaders, which has modelled effective leadership on the distinction between 'transactional' and 'transformational' styles of leadership (e.g. Vinnicombe and Singh 2002).

Originally introduced in the work of Burns (1978), and developed by Rosener (1990), a 'transformational' leader is one who can transform and is able to motivate subordinates to transform their own self-interest into the interest of the group through concern for a broader goal. This is achieved through enthusiasm, energy, engagement, sharing power and information and encouraging participation. Following this, Vinnicombe and Singh (2002) describe a woman's management and communication style as being based on personal respect, mutual trust, regard for the contribution that each team member can bring, and the development of the individual and diverse talent. However, the term 'transformational' has since developed broader connotations (see Chapter 3 for discussion), so in line with Fletcher (1999), Holmes (2006) and others, a more precise term to describe the female leadership style for the purposes of this book is 'relational'. This is set in contrast to the traditional 'transactional leader', who views job performance as a series of transactions with subordinates – exchanging rewards for services rendered or punishment for inadequate performance. In line with this, Vinnicombe and Singh (2002) describe a man's management and communication style as being reliant on power, position and formal authority. Such views were institutionalised for a time within assessment mechanisms such as the Personality Attributes Questionnaire (PAQ) developed by Spence, Helmreich and Stapp (1975), which identified two dimensions of management: instrumentality and expressiveness.

An alternative, language-based way of conceptualising leadership is in terms of the way leaders *use* language. Leadership is almost literally 'constructed' through the *step-by-step choices* speakers make as they enact leadership in the course of key decision-making forums such as meetings. The value of this 'performative' perspective is that it perceives leaders' language as vital for establishing their level of influence over colleagues, in terms of whether they can persuade others to their point of view, and are taken seriously as key players in the organisation. Every time a leader speaks, they are making a linguistic choice about how to perform leadership, and indeed, every time they open their mouths, they are being judged – but not always positively! Their use of language is of course intimately bound up with the exercise of power, and with colleagues' perceptions of how well they exercise this authority. Every interaction in a meeting or elsewhere in the workplace involves people enacting, reproducing and sometimes resisting institutional relationships by their careful use of a range of coercive and collaborative strategies (Holmes and Stubbe 2003). Furthermore, leadership is never a solo performance but jointly constructed. Senior people work together to construct effective or less effective leadership, and it is enacted through relationships involving different levels of acquiescence and resistance. Networking, negotiation, problem-solving and decision-making are central elements in this process. Fundamental aspects of linguistic behaviour such as the exercise of authority, the role of politeness and humour are often cleverly interwoven to produce an effective language of leadership (Holmes and Stubbe 2003; Schnurr 2008).

Of course, such a micro-analysis of the linguistic strategies used to achieve effective leadership is not sufficient on its own. The language of leadership is moderated too by institutional discourses within a business setting. These discourses may be 'gendered', possibly making simplistic 'sexist' assumptions about women leaders. It is important to look at 'gendered discourses' because they can have enormous implications for a woman's experience of leadership, and whether her leadership is deemed successful or otherwise. Discourses determine how possible it is for a senior woman to be evaluated positively by her colleagues and to be regarded as an influential role model to more junior colleagues.

Gendered discourses

The phrase 'gendered discourses' contains two strongly debated words that will crop up repeatedly throughout this book so it is clearly important to define both 'gender' and 'discourse'. The term 'gender' must be distinguished from 'sex', a well recognised sociolinguistic and grammatical term that is used to refer to the categories denoted by biological characteristics, such as the 'male sex' or the 'female sex' (Holmes 2001; Trudgill 2000). The term 'gender', in contrast, tends to imply a socio-cultural construct. 'Gender' usually refers to cultural constructions of what it means to be a sexed individual in the 21st century western world. When we discuss 'femininity' or 'feminine' styles of speech, we are therefore referring not to innate characteristics of being female, but the cultural associations with being a woman, which of course vary from one culture to another, one historical period to another. In this book I will adhere to the sex/gender distinction for its clarity and simplicity, while acknowledging the more controversial debate that has suggested that 'sex' is also a sociocultural construct (e.g. Bergvall, Bing and Freed 1996; Butler 1990; Cameron 2003). Such theorists argue that both the categories of sex and gender might be reconceptualised as a *continuum* or as scales rather than absolute categories. Indeed, this notion of a sex/gender continuum, rather than the polarisation of male and female as distinct categories, forms a crucial element within some types of business and discourse communities, as I describe further below.

The term 'discourse' is used widely and in different ways across academic disciplines and is often left undefined (Litosseliti 2006; Mills 1997). There have been three working definitions of discourse in recent years (Cameron 2001). First, traditional linguists tend to categorise discourse at the basic level as 'language above the sentence', a stretch of connected utterances or sentences. The mission of these linguists is to analyse discourse as texts with patterns and rules of coherence. Secondly, social scientists tend to regard discourse as 'language in use', as language with specific social functions such as institutional discourse, media discourse and educational discourse. Analysts working with this definition tend to look for distinct and predictable features and forms of expression within the different types of discourse. The third definition following Foucault (1972: 49) tends to view discourse in the plural as discour*ses*, as 'language that systematically forms the object of which it speaks'. In other words, discourses are 'language as social practices': a social construction of reality from a particular perspective, which draw upon a form of privileged knowledge or social and ideological practice. In this book, I will draw expediently upon the second, singular definition when I need to make use of a descriptive label such as 'institutional discourse', but I will primarily use the third, plural definition of 'discourses' when I refer to language as broader social practices. In Chapter 4, I discuss 'discourse theory', a key theoretical framework in this book, which helps to explain the dialogic process of how individuals both shape and are shaped by institutional ways of speaking and interacting with others. A key theme of this book however is the role of *gendered* discourses which, I argue, produce considerably more expectations and constraints upon the roles and performance of *female* than male leaders.

Gendered discourses are therefore the sets of attitudes and norms that operate within any organisation that conceptualise gender in hegemonic, male-dominated or gender-divided ways. Identifying a discourse, and what constitutes a discourse, is clearly an academic construct in itself. Sociolinguists who have identified 'gendered discourses' in particular have combined two key research methods: long-term ethnographic study of linguistic interactions in social contexts, and detailed micro-analysis of specific samples of language (e.g. Baxter 2003; Mullany 2007; Sunderland 2004). There is thus some empirical evidence upon which to argue that gendered discourses 'exist' and are a generally recognisable phenomenon. In this book, I will be examining a number of gendered discourses that have been identified and labelled by recent researchers (*op. cit.*) such as discourses of *gender difference, masculinisation* and *female emotionality* and *irrationality*.

Gendered discourses are particularly identifiable within linguistic contexts such as meetings where conflicts of interest between senior people may emerge. From a gender perspective, meeting time may be viewed as 'a contested space' in which women struggle at times to have their views heard, valued and acted upon (Holmes 2006). Holmes has argued that 'gendered norms of workplace talk can subtly contribute to excluding women from positions of power and influence' (2006: 33). I have shown in my own work (Baxter 2003), that women leaders have an equal if not a greater chance to speak than their male counterparts, but there are ways in which their contributions are subtly undermined. For example, the way senior women are sometimes characterised by others: as *scary, bossy, hard, tough, mean, bullying, moody, irrational, bitchy,* and so on, may infiltrate a meeting context in an implied rather than a stated way by means of a joke made at a woman's expense, which provokes general laughter. But for a woman the joke isn't always funny, even if she laughs along with everyone else. Is she just being humourless? Perhaps. After all, there are always going to be jokes at people's expense, as much against men as women. And learning to be good-humoured on such occasions is of course a trick of the trade. But it is on occasions such as these that gendered discourses may undermine the effectiveness of senior women's contributions to meetings, simply because there isn't an equivalent supply of sexist jokes directed against senior men. However, there is also evidence in my own data of female excellence as speakers when they show their colleagues just how to 'do the language of leadership' (see Chapter 6). Enacting authority in order to get business done expertly can be achieved by a finely nuanced range of linguistic skills, and women leaders are often particularly effective at using these. This linguistic expertise is one of the various ways in which senior women can work to counter the effect of gendered discourses within their corporation.

Gendered corporations

Based on my own research experience (Baxter 2003, 2008), there appears to be a key relationship between the degree of success that senior women may attain at leadership level and the type of corporation they work for. Kanter (1977) was one of the first to suggest that all corporations are fundamentally *gendered*. A 'gendered corporation' is partly a product of gendered discourses circulating within that organisation, and partly a systematic means of producing and sustaining them. Bargiela-Chiappini and Harris (1997: 4) have claimed that:

> Organisations are talked into being and maintained by means of talk of the people within and around them. Among the 'competing discourses' that shape daily organisational life, some become dominant.

Just as discourses about gender circulate in the broader social world, some of which have a strong influence upon people's frames of reference, so such discourses will permeate the workplace and operate in similar but more contained and culture-specific ways. Indeed, a particular type of gendered discourse – one based on the belief of the existence of *gender difference* – will have certain expectations of the ways in which males and females should speak, behave and interact within a corporation.

Refining the work of Kanter (1977) and others, I suggest that there are three prototypical gendered corporations, each of which privileges a dominant gendered discourse: *Male-Dominated, Gender-Divided* and *Gender-Multiple*. In my view, a woman who works for a Male-Dominated corporation is likely to have a far more difficult experience of leadership than a colleague who works for a more supportive, Gender-Multiple corporation, so it matters which type of corporation a woman joins!

In order to provide a theoretical basis for this schematisation and explore their impact on women leaders, I intend to link these three types of gendered corporation to three major theories within the field of Gender and Language: dominance, difference and discourse theories (see Litosseliti 2006, for fuller expositions). While I make no attempt to suggest a *causal* relationship between the theory and the type of corporation, there is nevertheless a rich connection to be made between the explanatory power of the theory and its realisation as a set of linguistic and professional practices within a corporation. Arguably, an *actual* company will incorporate elements of all three types of community, but I suggest that one of the three types is likely to figure more predominantly and characterise a female leader's experience within it.

To help identify each type of gendered corporation as the framework for my subsequent analysis, I have set out below a brief description of the structural, cultural and linguistic features pertaining to each.

The Male-Dominated corporation

This type of gendered corporation is characterised by its allegiance to a patriarchal view of gender relationships in which societies are unequally divided on gender lines in such a way that the male sex of the species is considered to be superior in strength, intellect and other survival and social skills, whereas the female sex of the species is subordinate in all these respects. This perspective was reinforced by traditional, anthropological studies that examined the division of labour of the sexes into male/public and female/private spheres, and by the way this was reflected in language use (see Cameron 1992 for an overview). Unquestionably, there are parts of the world where the social organisation of communities and corporations still works along these lines – however outdated this appears to be from a western perspective. Despite the increasing unacceptability of a male dominance perspective in the western world, I suggest that there are residual and sometimes overt elements of masculinised language practices in many corporations today.

The 'dominance' theory in Language and Gender literature (e.g. Fishman 1978; Lakoff 1975; Spender 1980) puts forward the view that there is an unequal division of labour in the way that males and females conduct conversations, which actually serves to construct and reinforce the division of power in male and female relationships. So males tend to use a range of dominance strategies in the way they speak such as using display talk, interrupting others, telling extended jokes, not listening, boasting, using verbal harassment, accusations, insults and put-downs, whereas females tend to use a range of supportive strategies such as careful listening, agreement, use of minimal responses (*yes, OK, go on*), questions and tag questions to encourage the conversation of men. The dominance theory has also investigated the perceived use of sexist language to describe women in power, which is often invoked in cases of sexual harassment (Spender 1980; Litosseliti 2006). Such studies aimed to expose the male bias in language (indicated by the use of generics such as 'he' for 'he/she'; lexical terms of address such as 'chairman' rather than 'chairperson'; derogatory terms for women as 'babes', and so on).

How is such social and linguistic evidence of male and female inequality manifested in the Male-Dominated corporation? This type of discourse community considers that males are the natural-born leaders and that women provide an excellent support and back-up service. This is reflected in their respective speech styles where men use language in clear, direct, authoritative and sometimes aggressive ways, whereas women are expected to be supportive conversationalists backing the authority, views and ideas of men. Men use speech to command and control, to get access to the floor, and once there, to keep it. They are likely to use language for display purposes, asserting their dominance through verbosity, name-dropping, subtle or overt boasting, and entertainment strategies such as jokes and anecdotes. Women on the other hand are expected to listen and to be amused by men. On the whole, they are expected to agree and support, and not to interrupt, challenge or question the authority of men. If they do challenge, they will need to do this in acceptable ways in order not to upset the *status quo*.

There is a 'reconstructed' version of the Male-Dominated corporation which would be much more recognisable to people today, given that very few companies wish to be seen as overtly male-dominated and indeed, have diversity policies and practices in place. In Chapter 2, I discuss how the reconstructed version operates under the guise of *gender-neutrality*, in which senior women and men might argue quite vociferously that there are no forms of discrimination practised against women (or any other perceived minority). The principle here is that of a *meritocracy*: that any individual can achieve success on the grounds of merit and hard work, and that there are always instances of female leaders, or people from different ethnic minorities, who illustrate the principle (Rojo and Esteban 2003). The evidence that gender-neutrality is masking a Male-Dominated corporation in these settings is often manifested by means of *tokenism* (Kanter 1977): the presence of just *one* woman (or member of an ethnic minority) on the main board, and very few women at a lower senior management level. Brewis (2001) argues that another strong sign of a Male-Dominated corporation masquerading as a gender-neutral community is where there is prevalent use of negative or sexist language (by both men and women) to describe female leaders as 'scary', 'bossy', 'hard', 'a man in woman's clothes', and so on.

The Gender-Divided corporation

Men are from Mars and Women are from Venus.

(John Gray 1992)

The Gender-Divided corporation is based on an allegiance to one of the most pervasive and traditional gendered discourses: the gender difference view that there are two sexes, distinctly polarised into male and female categories, but considered to be different yet *equal*. So in contrast to a 'dominance' view of women as deficient or subordinate, women's perceived biological, cultural and linguistic differences from men are positively valued and even celebrated (e.g. Coates 1996; Tannen 1994b). Such a revaluation has been theorised in anthropological studies of males and females, which has conceptualised the sexes as members of different 'sub-cultures' (Maltz and Borker 1982). According to this, males and females are gradually socialised from childhood into two separate sex-role sub-cultures with different but perhaps complementary behavioural and conversational goals. So boys use aggressive language because their goal is to assert themselves, and girls use co-operative language because they want to make close friends and be sociable. Thus boys and girls learn to use the same language differently through their play and learning in single-sex peer groups. The 'gender difference' view has had a huge effect upon a range of social science disciplines such as psychology, sociology, organisational behaviour and education, as well as on the common-sense thinking of the general public. It has produced a multi-million pound self-help industry trading on the idea that males and females might as well come from different planets (Gray 1992; Pease and Pease 2001; Tannen 1990, 1994).

The 'difference' theory in Language and Gender literature (e.g. Coates 2004; Holmes 1995; Tannen 1990) has taken a feminist perspective on the perceived difference in male and female linguistic styles. Tannen (1990) has argued that the perceived male preference for 'report talk' (goal-orientated, direct, assertive, confrontational) complements the female preference for 'rapport talk' (co-operative, supportive, indirect and engaging), and that both types of speech style have their place in work and social contexts. Such theorists have advocated that women can lead the way in expressing more effective ways of communicating (Coates 1995; Holmes 2006; Schnurr 2008), a theme also taken up by organisational behaviourists in relation to leadership (e.g. Anderson, Vinnicombe and Singh 2008; Helgesen 1990; Olsson 2006). However, difference in gender-based speech styles can also lead to miscommunication and misunderstandings between the sexes. Much of the popular literature has focused on this element, but in a male-centred way by suggesting that women should increase their linguistic awareness of male communication styles in order to understand them better, and so to prevent the breakdown of personal and professional relationships.

Thus, in the Gender-Divided corporation, men are expected to be more competitive while women are assumed to be more co-operative. Males and females adopt different roles in the organisation: males tend to dominate at senior management levels, although there are token women, more at middle than at senior level, while women occupy most of the administrative and clerical posts because they are deemed to be better equipped for these roles. Women are of course appreciated for the roles they fulfil, but may find it difficult to 'break through the glass ceiling' because they are not considered to be 'leadership material'. Where miscommunication does occur between the sexes that might lead to conflicts, the organisation has trained both males and females in the linguistic strategies needed to 'read' the intentions of the 'opposite' sex. In enlightened versions of this type of discourse community, senior women are explicit about the value of the feminine aspects of their leadership styles and put these into action. This type of community is likely to encourage the use of 'relational' styles of leadership, which support the practice of social engagement, openness, participation, sharing of power, and a stronger sense of team. The 'downside' of the Gender-Divided corporation is that comparisons may be made between the two different styles which can lead to negative judgements about the quality of one style over the other. As 'relational' styles of leadership are associated more with putting people first rather than a cold focus on profit, they are not likely to be valued as highly as 'transactional' styles. Where gendered discourses also circulate about the possible weaknesses of the feminine style, it may be hard for senior women to demonstrate that the feminine style of speech or the relational style of leadership is different but equal in its value and impact.

The Gender-Multiple corporation

This third type of corporation in my typology is based on the cultural view that gender plays a strong part in the lives of people but isn't necessarily an all-defining feature governing the way people speak and behave. In this corporation, people's identities are viewed as a fluid mix of gender, age, education, professional status, ethnicity, language, class, personality and so on. In other words, difference and diversity are essential to the way people distinguish themselves. Femininity (or masculinity) is seen as multi-dimensional rather than defined solely by gender constructs or narrow stereotypes. Women for example can embrace and incorporate the often contradictory positions in their lives: as professionals, career women, friends of other women and men, colleagues, mothers, lovers, wives, partners and daughters. In this corporation, there are flexible definitions of gender and sexuality, such that both aspects of identity would be viewed in terms of continua or overlapping categories rather than as binary oppositions. This contrasts with a gender-neutral corporation (often a 'mask' for a Male-Dominated corporation as we saw earlier, which dismisses gender's relevance to business and leadership practice).

In the Gender-Multiple corporation, there are relatively equal numbers of men and women at executive and managerial levels, and across the business functions. There isn't a preponderance of women at administrative and clerical levels, and men feel equally welcome to apply for such posts. Females are welcome and supported at board level, mentoring of able women is encouraged, and opportunities for promotion are organised according to well established diversity policies and career progression routes.

The discourse approach to language and gender is well placed to theorise and ratify the ethos of the Gender-Multiple corporation. This approach (Baxter 2003; Butler 1990; Crawford 1995) argues primarily that our gender is enacted through *performance* – both through speech and behaviour. In other words, it is not a case that we *are* a man or a woman, but that we construct and *perform* being a man or a woman through our actions and words. We *talk* our gender into being (Crawford 1995). Gender as it is enacted through speech is perceived as just one element – albeit a crucial one – of our multiple identities. Thus, interactional and speech styles reflect and construct the notion of gender multiplicity. In the case of leaders, both male and females are generally skilled enough to use a wide repertoire of speech styles traditionally coded 'masculine' and 'feminine' according to their conversational goals (Cameron 1997). They are readily able to switch between one type of code and another in order to perform transactional and relational functions. So, there is little discernible difference between the speech styles and males and the speech styles of females.

In this context, senior women are linguistic experts who know the power of language and are able to apply it to achieve effective leadership in their organisations. They are aware that 'gendered discourses' pervade their organisation and society generally, which could limit their effectiveness, but they are prepared to make these discourses explicit, and question them openly and critically in different forums.

This level of linguistic sophistication and awareness of gender discourses is found, in my experience, to be a relatively rare phenomenon. The Male-Dominated corporation (and some readers may find this hard to believe!) still plays a significant part in mainstream business practice as I now demonstrate.

2
Speaking in the Male-Dominated Corporation

Think manager, think male.

(Schein 1975)

I doubt that any business today would openly describe itself as a Male-Dominated corporation, and many senior people might say 'that's ancient history and we're not like that!' Over 30 years of equal opportunities and laws against sex discrimination have ensured that most businesses in the 21st century would say they openly support and encourage women's careers.

Yet, in my experience the Male-Dominated corporation continues to exist today, especially in banking, finance, insurance, building and engineering sectors (Baxter 2009). A male-dominated approach may not wholly characterise an organisation, but certain elements may feature in an informal or covert way. For example, senior women may be routinely talked about and represented negatively by colleagues – through small talk, gossip, jokes, anecdotes and informal discussions. Over time, if such negative stereotyping goes unchallenged, it is gradually institutionalised in the form of 'gendered discourses': prejudicial assumptions about women. Furthermore, many Male-Dominated corporations have attempted to reconstruct themselves in response to mainstream discourses of gender equality, and now go under the guise of a 'gender-neutral' corporation, but this is a pretence, as I shall discuss.

The Male-Dominated corporation

So what are the features of the *classic* Male-Dominated corporation? Principally, it upholds the view that males are the natural-born

23

leaders and that women provide an excellent support service. This is reflected in their respective speech styles where men use language in clear, direct, authoritative and sometimes aggressive ways, whereas women are expected to be supportive conversationalists backing the authority, views and ideas of men. Men use speech to command and control, to get access to the floor, and once there, to keep it. They are likely to use language for display purposes, asserting their dominance through verbosity, name-dropping, subtle or overt boasting, and entertainment strategies such as jokes and anecdotes. Women on the other hand are expected to listen and to be amused by men. On the whole, they are expected to agree and support, not to interrupt, challenge or question the authority of men. If they do challenge, they will need to do this in acceptable ways in order not to upset the *status quo*. This type of corporation is not a welcoming or comfortable one for female leaders. Women leaders may stand out as different and exceptional in the way they speak and behave, but in many ways this will work against them.

If the Male-Dominated corporation continues to exist in today's world, how is this manifested through language? By reviewing what past literature has to say and linking this with current research, this chapter will assess the extent to which leadership language remains masculinised and the property of males in current businesses.

Linguistic construction of leadership

Within many traditional models of leadership, the necessary and desirable qualities of being an effective leader have long been assumed to be masculine (Still 2006). This assumption is so deeply entrenched in western thinking and language that leadership often matches and mirrors the language of masculinity to reflect qualities such as aggressiveness, assertiveness, abrasiveness and competitiveness. In terms of career development and progression, 'corporate masculinity' operates as a norm that all managers aspiring to the top must adopt, whether male or female.

Schein's (1975) principle of 'think manager think male' goes far deeper than the obvious fact that women have been historically absent from business leadership positions and continue today to constitute a small minority on corporate boards worldwide. Classical Greek philosophers such as Aristotle, Plato and Socrates originally thought personal characteristics were important for leadership and proposed 'the great man' theory, which later evolved into the supreme trait of leadership. Leadership was assumed to be a property of the individual, involving superior genes or that magic ingredient, 'charisma'.

Investigating Australian corporate culture, Sinclair (1994, 1998) found that the 'great man' or 'hero' still dominated the criteria for leadership positions. Anyone embarking on a mission to gain membership of the executive culture was considered to be on 'a Ulysses-like journey full of grand-scale trials of endurance and tests of strength – the modern day equivalent of the heroic quest!' (Sinclair 1994: 15). As well as Ulysses on his 20-year epic journey, she points to heroes such as Theseus killing the Minotaur and Mercury the winged messenger – heroes with 'an archetypal profile'. Indeed, in the history of literature, there are numerous examples of male heroes showing courage and 'charisma' in the face of adversity. The leading characters in William Shakespeare's 'history' plays, always male and often of noble birth, appear in military settings leading their troops, or inspiring their followers to support them by force of persuasive rhetoric. Mark Antony's famously charismatic and manipulative speech in *Julius Caesar* (1599):

> Friends, Romans, Countrymen, lend me your ears
> I come to praise Caesar not to bury him

exhibits the close relationship between male leadership and the power of language to persuade doubters to his cause. This historical equation between leadership and being a persuasive public speaker continues today. The inauguration of Barrack Obama as American President in 2009 raises questions about his selection over his Democratic Party rival, Hillary Clinton. While many reasons may explain Obama's greater popularity over the female candidate, the powerful association of masculinity with the extraordinary gift for crowd-pleasing oratory continues to be viewed as a qualification for effective leadership (Cameron 2006).

In keeping with historical notions of leadership, the political economist Max Weber (1947) proposed three basic forms of authority. First, leadership may be seen as arising from the traditional authority that comes from a socially accepted status such as a father or King. Second, leadership may be understood as the product of the qualities and charisma of 'great men'. Third, leadership may be taken for granted as the usual complement of rational-legal authority within bureau-cracies, which might be seen as a means of legitimising and enfor-cing the power of 'great men'.

Connecting the history of leadership is the theme of the 'personality cult' or 'charisma': having a strong personal influence over others. A charismatic leader is defined by 'his' psychological qualities, in parti-cular by the ability to influence and persuade his followers. While as we shall see, the charismatic model has been firmly challenged by modern leadership theories and practices, researchers such as Rojo and Esteban (2003: 245) note that 'both in training materials and everyday discourses in organisations, an up-to-date version of the charismatic leader is still present in every personality profile of a leader offered by the different typologies of leadership we have found'. Of course, there is no reason to suppose that 'charisma' is usually perceived as the exclusive property of males. However, two sources of evidence sug-gest this may be the case. In a recent study of leadership 'role models' by Singh, Vinnicombe and James (2006), the authors found that young women managers admired 'charisma' in both male and female role models, although this was rather differently defined in each case. Yet the authors also found that 'women at the top' were often *rejected* as role models by these younger women because they 'were seen as having given up an essential part of their emotional and social capital to achieve success on masculine terms' (2006: 70). In the second source of evidence, a TV documentary entitled 'The Lost Art of Oratory' (BBC2 2009), it was proposed that being a 'charismatic speaker' was essential to outstanding leadership. Only two of the 15 examples of great leaders supplied by the programme were in fact female – Queen Elizabeth 1 and Margaret Thatcher.

While nothing is 'proved' by this evidence, what is certain is that the concept of charisma is still inextricably associated with leader-ship, and that leadership is routinely perceived as male. Indeed Rosabeth Moss Kanter (1977) in her classic work *Men and Women of the Corporation* notes that 'a masculine ethic' has always been part of the image of a good manager. This ethic:

> elevates the traits assumed to belong to men to necessities for effective management: a tough-minded approach to problems;

analytic abilities to abstract and plan; a capacity to set aside personal, emotional considerations in the interests of task accomplishment....These characteristics supposedly belonged to men; but then all managers were men from the beginning.

(Kanter 1977: 22–23)

Tough-minded....analytic abilities....task accomplishment: the 'masculine ethic' is realised in so many ways through the sustaining and reinforcing medium of language. It is to the various ways in which language actually constructs a masculinised organisational culture that I now turn.

Masculinised cultures

Masculine definitions of leadership are connected to a masculine ethic in the workplace which in turn interacts with the 'organisational culture' in which people move. Definitions of what is meant by 'organisational cultures' within the context of gender have been keenly debated (e.g. Halford and Leonard 2001; Legge 1995; Liff and Cameron 1997; Pemberton 1995), and it is not my purpose to reinvent the wheel here. But briefly, Halford and Leonard (2001) identify two main approaches to understanding the concept: first, culture as a variable – that is, something that an organisation *has* – and secondly, culture as a root metaphor – something an organisation *is* and *does*. For our purposes, the second of the two definitions of culture is more in harmony with our social constructionist understanding of language in organisations, in that it emphasises how attitudes, norms and values become institutionalised within business and leadership practices:

[The] organisation is a subjective experience and therefore the purpose of studying an organisation is to discover the shared cognitions and beliefs; to understand the rules that collective minds have generated and which guide action.

(Pemberton 1995: 113)

According to this approach, therefore, culture is both 'the shaper of human action and the outcome of a process of social creation and reproduction' (Legge 1995: 186). Of particular interest here are the ways in which a corporate culture may have a gendered basis, or be infused by particular gendered discourses, either in the broader organisation as a whole or within smaller, sub-divided groups. A Male-Dominated corporation is likely to be masculinised in ethic and outlook, either manifestly, implicitly or residually, although this could take a variety of forms.

> *The Gentleman's Club*: polite, civilised; women kept in established roles offering them few opportunities; and patronises them, but courteously. According to this traditional ethic, women are pressurised into feeling they have too much to lose if they challenge male superiors; women are valued and treated with respect on the basis that they don't move out of traditional roles or functions. The 'old boy network' features in this type of culture, where men provide other men who are known to them from a shared school or university background with opportunities for promotion and achievement. The language of the gentleman's club would be for men to treat women with polite, old-fashioned, paternalist courtesy, and to treat other men either combatively or with jocular abuse.

> *The Barrack Yard*: these are hierarchical organisations which have a strict chain of command from top to bottom. This is an authoritarian culture where overt power commands respect. Within this culture, women may be ignored or rendered invisible. Women who challenge the order are regarded as a threat and may be sidelined as a consequence. As this may be a bullying culture, linguistic interaction would take the form of direct orders, a lack of politeness and on occasions, shouting and verbal abuse.

Figure 2.1   Masculinised cultures: overt

Maddock and Parkin (1993) devised a colourful typology of 'gendered cultures', based on extensive 'equality audits' they carried out in the UK in the early 1990s, which they found to describe and define the dominant processes, practices, attitudes and values of many of the organisations they investigated. The two overtly male-dominated, gendered cultures in Figure 2.1 are a relatively rarity in western corporations today, in my experience, but strongly indicate where we have come from historically. Adding to Maddock and Parkin's (*ibid*) model on p. 28, I have commented on the linguistic implications of each type of culture.

Other gendered cultures which are male-dominated may be far less overt and unsubtle, in the view of Maddock and Parkin (1993), but they are nonetheless inscribed by a deeply entrenched, masculinised world-view. These are cultures that may strongly purport to be gender-inclusive, and where women work on a relatively equal footing to men. On paper, there are equal opportunities for women, and there are females at senior level. Indeed, employees may perceive themselves as working within a relatively 'gender-neutral' culture where both females and males vouch that there is little if any discrimination in the organisation, and that it is down to personal effort and ability to succeed. Maddock and Parkin (1993) suggest that the following four types of organisation exhibit covert, male-dominated cultures as shown in Figure 2.2.

At first glance, the Locker room gender culture (see overleaf) might seem to pertain more to 'overt' than to 'covert' male-dominated cultures, but I have found evidence of it even in the most avowedly forward-looking and diversity-sensitive companies. In some research I conducted in a well-known UK internet company comprising equal numbers of male and female employees (Baxter 2003), the only woman on the executive board, who was in fact the founder member of this company, complained in an interview with me that she often felt excluded from the 'boysy' ('boy-like') culture of her male colleagues:

> I think the reason why I've been feeling defensive lately is because of the feeling that I'm being marginalised by that boysy culture that I have nothing much to contribute to it.

> (Baxter 2003: 166)

One of the consequences of male-dominated cultures within many western corporations is that they offer only a limited range of

➢ *The Locker Room*: an exclusion culture where men build relationships in unofficial ways on the basis of common agreements, assumptions and shared interests such as sport, entertainment, and sexual references. For men there would be informal meetings in pubs, golf clubs, bars, restaurants, and shared sport activities. Women leaders may feel isolated and 'left out' of this masculinised culture. Between men, the language of interaction would involve sexist language, sexual references, innuendo and banter, as well as bodily 'display' behaviour in meetings. With women, men might use flirtatious language which has the risk of being interpreted as sexual harassment.

➢ *The Gender Blind*: an apparently gender-neutral culture that denies that there are issues of gender discrimination; a 'level playing field' that encourages people actively to dismiss the significance of gender at work. This may have the unintended effect of encouraging women to aspire to superwoman status in order to prove that they are as good as men in a manís world. Thus, women often have to be exceptional in order to survive in this type of culture. Women tend to use a more masculinised language: assertive, direct, combative with the occasional swear words for emphasis and effect.

➢ *The Feminist Pretenders*: this view plays lip-service to equal opportunities and can even be stridently, politically correct. People who do not conform to the alternative stereotypes face their own form of victimisation. As it is rarely based on genuine equality of respect or real human values, it encourages a culture of blame. The language of this culture would be politically correct: *Chair* for *chairperson*, *Ms* instead of *Miss/Mrs*, and so on.

➢ *The Smart Macho*: driven wholly by business values: competition; efficiency; cost-saving; making profits; over-work; sacrifice. Superficially the culture is gender-blind treating everyone as equals. Usually involves younger, single, childless, metro-sexual people, both male and female, who are encouraged to be self-centred and egoistic. But for women it may be far more difficult to sustain this type of lifestyle because arguably they are also socialised to orient to the needs of others (Maltz and Borker 1982). The language for both males and females would be very similar, with an emphasis on the transactional goals of the organisation: direct, functional, business-like, a use of masculinised metaphors (see below), politically correct.

Figure 2.2   Masculinised cultures: covert

approved roles for women leaders, many of which are 'semantically derogated' (Schulz 1975); that is, they have negative connotations. Continuing the jargon, there is often a 'negative semantic space' (Spender 1980: 20) for women leaders in Male-Dominated corporations. In order to show how gendered cultures are often enacted through language, I shall now discuss linguistic terms used in organisations to describe women – from a 'dominance theory' perspective (see Chapter 1).

Terms for women

How do women leaders survive and fit into Male-Dominated corporations? One way is by taking up one of a very limited number of possible roles and positions which have been deemed acceptable by that gendered culture, but these have implications for the way women use language, and the way language is used *about* them and sometimes *against* them.

Sex-role stereotyping has been identified as a problem for women managers (e.g. Vinnicombe and Singh 2002). When women gain positions or power in the Male-Dominated corporation, there are a limited number of identity roles they can adopt which enables them to conduct their professional roles legitimately. Such roles have a value in that they give women a 'security of place' and are used to routinise interactions between men and women in traditional settings. But because these roles are limited and easily definable, they are also exposed to negative stereotyping which is transmitted through language.

'Dominance' theory (e.g. Schulz 1975; Spender 1980) considered that many of the terms available to describe women and their experiences are gender-biased or 'sexist'. This stemmed from the radical feminist view that the language we all speak has evolved historically to reflect and construct patriarchal norms: that is, the centrality of male experiences and perspectives. In line with this 'androcentric' world-view, terms to denote the male experience are unmarked as 'normal', whereas terms to denote the female experience are marked as abnormal, exceptional or deviant. A number of areas of language use were flagged up by 'dominance' researchers for attention. One of them was the problematic use of pronouns, particularly the generic use of 'he', 'him' and 'his' to refer to both men and women, as well as 'man/mankind' and expressions like 'man in the street'. Another was quite simply the labels used to describe women ranging from apparently straightforward terms like 'girl', 'lady', 'mistress' or 'madam' to terms marked with suffices such as 'act*ress*', 'host*ess*', 'manag*eress*' and so on. Such terms to denote females were often considered to be 'semantically derogated': that is, they had acquired negative and disparaging meanings over time, and in the case of words like 'mistress' and 'madam' had become sexualised. Feminist linguists like Schulz (1975) argued that almost any term used to describe women would eventually become 'contaminated' and incur sexual or derogatory meanings. She pointed out an apparent double standard in the use of language: terms that are neutral when applied to a man, become semantically derogated when applied to a woman.

This tendency in the history of language to semantically derogate women brings a new dimension to Kanter's (1977) classic work in which she mapped out four highly limited and sexualised roles available to women leaders (the Mother, Seductress, Pet and Iron Maiden). I shall re-examine this range of roles from a *linguistic* perspective, in order to consider the implications of this form of 'role-based' semantic derogation within the Male-Dominated corporation:

The Mother*:* This term implies that women leaders give emotional support and care for their subordinates. While it has powerful connotations within a domestic setting, it is a more disempowered role within professional and business settings. 'The mother' would be expected to take the role of comforter and sympathiser to both men and women. They are the ones to whom people bring family-related problems or difficulties with relationships that may be impinging on work life. The problem with this role is that women may be associated more with socio-emotional than professional expertise. Words used to describe this role-type such as 'motherly', 'maternal', 'soft', 'kind', 'caring' and 'nurturing' is likely to neutralise 'the mother' as a sexual threat to men, but invite suggestions that such women are potentially subordinate, and can be readily overruled by male/paternal authority.

An instance of the mother as leadership role is to be found in Wodak's (1997) case study research on three female head teachers. She concludes that all of her case study subjects adopted the mother role, perhaps because it meshed with the pastoral responsibility of looking after schoolchildren. But she also found that the three women used the role in differing ways to apply 'controlling and authoritarian strategies to achieve their aims which they sometimes take from the mother's repertoire of rules' (Wodak 1997: 367). One wonders whether Wodak's own description of these women's leadership strategies doesn't contribute to the negative evaluation of women in power.

The second role Kanter (1977) identified for female leaders was a highly sexualised one:

> **The Seductress:** This term implies that women leaders are primarily evaluated according to their sexual attractiveness and their interest in seducing men, and so closely fits with the semantically derogated perspective of women outlined above. This role-type may be consciously or unconsciously adopted but either way is problematic for the way female leaders are perceived. According to Kanter (1977: 234), if a senior woman is assumed to be sharing her attention too widely, she 'risks the debasement of whore'. If she risks giving her attention to one man above others, she arouses resentment and suspicion and may be driven out of the organisation. This is apparently because the seductress is able to form an alliance with one very senior man within the organisation, which may arouse jealousy and suspicion in their male colleagues. Regardless, women who play this role are usually perceived as a threat, which may mean they receive a good deal of attention (sexual rather than professional), or conversely, are avoided and marginalised. While there is little research to support how male leaders speak of such women because this would be seen as highly taboo, it can be speculated, based on legal cases of sexual harassment, that words of a derogatory sexual nature may well be applied. Indeed, the seductress role is not only a threat to men, but also to other women. Female leaders can find that they are ostracised by their female peers socially.

An instance of the seductress as leadership role is to be found in Olsson and Walker's (2003) interview-based research with New Zealand female executives. She found that (the now rather outdated phrase) 'the dolly bird' was used by female executives as a term of abuse against other women:

> When you enter a business environment, it's actually a negative, because there is a strong stereotypical dolly bird and unfortunately there are women who have used that image to attain power, to attain positions. And there are a lot of intelligent women out there – it doesn't do well for those women when it happens.
>
> (Olsson 2003: 6)

The third role Kanter (1977) identified for female leaders was a homely and infantilising one:

> **The Pet:** This term implies that the 'pet', who is adopted by her male colleagues as 'a cute amusing little thing' (Kanter 1977: 235), is not treated seriously as an equal. Pets can often have a great sense of humour and be 'one of the boys', but they are tolerated as a form of amusement rather than accepted. Halford and Leonard (2001: 109) suggest that this encourages 'a kind of look-what-she-did-and-she's only a woman' attitude, which is ultimately disempowering for women. It can involve a teasing relationship where there is mock-abuse. It can also be a mask for tokenism: having chosen a token woman for the board, male leaders are unsure about how to deal with them on equal terms. Words used to describe pets are invariably infantilised and therefore patronising such as 'cute', 'sweet', 'funny', 'a laugh', 'endearing', 'a good sport', and so on. This connects with the androcentric principle in language (see above), which assumes the male to be the linguistic norm and treats the female as the marked or exceptional term.

An example of 'the Pet' as a perceived role model for female leaders is to be found in my own research (Baxter 2003), involving interviews with 20 senior men and women. One female Human Resources Director volunteered the implication that the Main Board saw her as their pet, and that she enjoyed this treatment:

> I have a very good relationship with Exco (Executive committee) and more than two of them will say, 'R. will bully us!' Me bully them when they are two levels above! I think it is quite an affec-

tionate form of teasing. I think they have given me permission to bully them and they tease me for it.

(Baxter 2003: 214)

Interestingly, the speaker has uncritically and almost fondly used the sexist term that has been used against her to characterise her authority as a woman. Yet, arguably, this female appropriation of a male world-view (unless done in a critical or satirical spirit) is unlikely to help women who are aiming for the top and intending to remain there on an equal basis with men. Accepting one's status as 'a pet' at board level can only confirm a woman's status as subordinate.

The fourth and final role Kanter (1977) identified for female leadership is perhaps the most used (and abused) by professional and laypeople alike:

Iron Maiden: This term (originally a medieval instrument of torture used against women) implies that women who refuse to take a more stereotypically feminised role are often viewed as unnaturally virilised, and this is therefore the most semantically derogated role of all. According to Kanter (*ibid*), iron maidens behave in tough, uncompromising and assertive ways traditionally associated with men. In the history of literature, women who have acted against type, have either met an untimely fate (for example, Shakespeare's Lady Macbeth), or were severely punished by their society (for example, Maggie Tulliver in George Eliot's *Mill on the Floss*). Iron Maidens refuse to take account of wider social discourses about gender that suggest that women are not supposed to speak and behave aggressively. If they are in male-dominated organisations, they will be particularly vilified and subjected to both male and female contempt. They receive *male* contempt because they haven't accepted their subordinate status and may be perceived as a competitive threat, and they receive *female* contempt because they are acting differently from other women in the organisation who have accepted their stereotypical status. Where 'iron maidens' have managed to assimilate themselves in male-dominated cultures, they may be re-appropriated as 'honorary men', regardless of their sexuality. Linguistically, they will be subject to a range of semantically derogated descriptions from others: *scary, tough, mean, hard, bullies, bitches, lesbians, feminists, dykes,* and so on.

Olsson and Walker (2003) found evidence of the Iron Maiden in their case studies of female executives in New Zealand. Women executives themselves were quite prepared to characterise their female colleagues in this way as one respondent illustrates:

> Some corporate women can be quite hard. We joke about them being corporate transvestites, because they look like women and dress like men.
>
> (Olsson and Walker 2003: 6)

Chase (1988: 285) has suggested that 'the iron maiden is of course suicidal in the context of the organisation. She makes trouble for others and hence is left without support'. This role, like the others, represents a simplistic or parodic version of a leadership role for women wishing to make their mark at senior level. The specific problem of the Iron Maiden, unlike the other roles, lies in the way that it appropriates qualities conventionally perceived as being masculine.

So we can see that the assumption that leadership is male is deeply entrenched in western cultures, and one of its implications for senior women is that it produces double standards in language use. Relatively positive (or at least conventional) qualities used to describe male leaders such as *aggression, assertiveness, abrasiveness* and *competitiveness* are translated into negative qualities when they are used to describe a woman. In the UK newspaper, *The Sunday Times* (Campbell and Watt 2007) which reported the sacking of Rachida Dati, the French Minister of Justice, one of the reasons given for dissatisfaction at her job performance was 'an abrasive management style'. Quite acceptable when applied to a man, the same phrase applied to a woman becomes a form of opprobrium. Furthermore, when women leaders demonstrate qualities stereotypically associated with men, a distortion of the language often occurs: the reasonably positive adjective *assertive* becomes *aggressive, bossy* or *strident*. The adjectives *aggressive, strident* and *shrill* were frequently applied to the speech of the UK Tory Prime Minister, Margaret Thatcher, and famously, she had to undergo speech training, a form of 'verbal hygiene' (Cameron 1995), to lower the pitch of her voice in order to sound more like a man. By adopting the *Pygmalion* principle ('why can't a woman be more like a man?' (Shaw 1916)), Thatcher's advisers considered that she was less likely to be negatively evaluated by the voting public. However, she also received much public opprobrium for doing so. Further ways senior women have found to regulate and correct their language use are examined in more detail in Chapter 5.

In sum, the Iron Maiden and other sex-role stereotypes suggest that leadership is not considered a female occupation in the Male-Dominated corporation. A female leader is regarded as an aberration and women who become leaders are offered the dubious accolade of being compared to male leaders, either because they appear very *like* men (the Iron Maiden) or very *unlike* men (the Mother, the Seductress, the Pet). We can see that the linguistic means by which female leaders appear to fulfil aberrant roles is through the use of metaphor – the metaphors used above connote the female as masculinised, sexualised or infantilised. Another way in which metaphor is used to construct a linguistic environment from which women leaders can feel excluded is through the use of war and sports metaphors.

Masculinised metaphors

The reason gendered cultures and sex-role stereotypes exist at all is that they are continuously reproduced through individual and group language use, and one significant way this happens is through masculinised metaphors.

Researchers of workplace discourse such as Koller (2004) have noted that war/fighting metaphors are by far the most frequently used, followed by sporting, games and mating metaphors. It is hardly surprising that *war* metaphors figure most prominently because, as Lakoff and Johnson (1980: 63–64) suggest somewhat androcentrically:

> Even if you have never fought a fistfight in your life, much less a war, but have been arguing from the time you began to talk, you still conceive of arguments, and execute them according to the 'argument is war' metaphor, because the metaphor is built into the conceptual system of the culture in which you live.

In a detailed study of business media discourse relating to mergers and acquisitions (M&A) and marketing, Koller (2004) found that war and sports metaphors were routinely interrelated in reports of competition between big multi-nationals. Scenarios either involved contenders moving aggressively in their fight over territory (war metaphor), or runners moving fast across a racing turf towards a finishing line (sports metaphor). Using examples from a range of UK business newspapers, Koller shows how the marketplace is reconstructed as 'a battleground' over which 'war has been declared'. Koller found that such phrases as 'battling for market share', engaging in 'a bruising turf war' or 'fighting a death struggle' were routinely invoked to convey the sense of strong competition between companies.

In my own research investigating what makes an effective leader (Baxter 2008), I found that male managers in particular drew upon an interconnected language of war and sport to articulate their experiences of leadership. However, it wasn't all about war and sport. My findings also showed that there appeared to be one set of metaphors (war) to describe the more 'transactional' side of business leadership and another (therapy) to describe the more 'transformational' aspects as this male leader reveals:

> I am in a tough market; you do get *price wars*; you do get *winners and losers*, and I can't *fight the world* outside, but how we *attack it* is that we do seek trust with each other, with our customers, our suppliers (metaphors italicised).
>
> (Baxter 2008: 216)

I will return in Chapter 4 to the intriguing way in which leadership language intermingles war metaphors with something more therapeutic ('seek trust with each other'). But a prevailing theme within this research, particularly when it came to describing what makes an effective leader, was to encode the experience in metaphorically masculine ways, as this female Vice-President's comment exhibits:

> I think there is a point when you have to be confrontational with someone making difficulties for you. You have to be prepared to make your point and *stand your ground*, even if you are *being attacked*.
>
> (Baxter 2008: 214)

Koller (2004: 5) is one of a number of researchers who argues that the way in which leadership language is constituted by war and sports metaphors helps to 'masculinise both that discourse and related social practices'. Since war can be considered a 'quintessentially masculine activity and an essential test of manhood' (Wilson 1992: 892), its metaphoric usage arguably helps to marginalise metaphoric femininity and consequently, position women as an 'out-group' in business. Repeated use of war metaphors, both in quantitative and qualitative terms help to 'strengthen[s] the individual's sense of maleness...and a predominantly male culture' (Wilson 1992: 898). War metaphors therefore serve an ideological function, and according to Connell (1995: 77) may well help 'the top levels of business [to] provide a fairly convincing display of corporate masculinity.' Koller (2004: 174) argues from a feminist perspective that living in a linguistic environment conceptualised metaphorically as highly aggressive, if not a war zone, may bring ethical problems in making it easier to accept behaviour 'such as unchecked ruthlessness and brutality'. Warming to her theme, Koller (*ibid*) argues that while there are many commendable qualities associated with soldiers of war, such as courage, will-power, clear decisions and actions, there are less benevolent states such as 'a paranoid worldview, black-and-white thinking, repression of fear, compassion and guilt, as well as obsession with rank and hierarchy, de-individualisation and outward direction of aggression.'

While there is an element of 'going over the top' in Koller's (2004) analysis, to continue the war analogy, she nevertheless makes a very valuable point about the ways in which gendered discourses are constructed, sustained and perpetuated through leadership and business language. In simpler terms, metaphor works 'below the radar' of many companies' diversity policies, and is so much part of 'business speak' that it wouldn't be noticed. However it can have a powerful role in sustaining the ethos of the Male-Dominated corporation.

As I said at the start of the chapter, very few companies today want to be seen as overtly masculinised. One of the ways in which Male-Dominated corporations have attempted to reconstruct themselves, is by *posing* as 'gender-neutral corporations'. As I consider gender neutrality to be a form of disguise, it is important that we now uncover the masculine ethos that lies beneath.

The gender-neutral guise

'I'm just someone in business who happens to be a woman.'
(Olsson and Walker 2003: 4)

A gender-neutral corporation is, in theory, one in which gender has ceased to be an issue, and as a consequence men and women are treated equally on the strength of their individual merits. Indeed, research (e.g. Baxter 2008; Chase 1988; Olsson and Walker 2003) indicates that many senior women perceive themselves as working within gender-neutral corporations, often because they see themselves as the success stories and living proof that sex discrimination cannot be an issue. Although there are undoubtedly contexts where gender-neutrality must feature, the claim for its wider existence in business organisations must be viewed with considerable scepticism. This is because it can be a covert instrument for maintaining and reproducing masculinised cultures, in my view, as the 'gender-blind' culture described on p. 30, indicates.

In their study of 30 female senior executives in New Zealand, Olsson and Walker (2003) found that all the women they interviewed downplayed gender as a factor in their career progression and when asked directly, denied that gender had affected the way they were viewed as leaders. A number of these women rejected the operation of a 'glass ceiling' in their own career experience, and perhaps implicitly differentiated themselves in this respect from less successful women, as in the case of this senior manager:

> People talk about glass ceilings for women and so on and so forth and I don't find it difficult to accept that it exists. I guess I don't recognise it for myself and therefore it doesn't exist for me.
>
> (Olsson and Walker 2003: 5)

In unpublished material from my own study (Baxter 2008), I found quite negative attitudes towards gender, implying that it was unnecessarily being 'talked up' in academic literature, but this was rather tellingly subverted in the 'iron maiden' analogy of the following respondent:

> In the end it's down to your own personality and your own strength of character to make a go of it. At the top, you've just got to have the balls.

Olsson and Walker (2003) argue that while most of their respondents tended to deny that gender was significant in their career progression, they also acknowledged the strong influence of male-dominated executive culture. Respondents signified this in incidental comments such as 'all my colleagues are men', 'my 100% male colleagues' and 'it's a little unusual to find a woman running a manufacturing company'. However, such self-referential comments might be partly accounted for by the fact that the respondents were aware that the researchers were investigating the position of women in their organisations. Olsson and Walker (2003) also noted that, when asked which individuals had given them most career assistance, most of the sample mentioned males rather than females as mentors. Again this might be explained by the statistical fact that the vast majority of corporations remain male-dominated at senior levels (Sealy, Vinnicombe and Singh 2008). However, at a time when many companies are concerned to promote female role models, one might reasonably expect to find some progress in this domain.

In a context where senior women are still firmly in the minority and have to forge their own way in an often hostile corporate world, why do successful women fail to acknowledge the distinctiveness of their position? Whether senior women are in a male-dominated company or a gender-multiple one (see Chapter 4), they are always going to be the 'marked' sex, linguistically and professionally, until such time as there are equal numbers of males and females in company boardrooms (Holmes 2006). As the marked sex, they continue to remain 'visible' in terms of their very presence and therefore available for comparison with their male peers (Kanter 1977).

Chase (1988: 280) has suggested that the reason why some senior women 'deny' their gender is exactly because they 'must work against a negative stereotype of women in general'. A woman must primarily establish herself as a professional and prove that she is more independent and productive than people expect women in general to be. The professional woman needs to prove that popular stereotypes about women in the workplace aren't necessarily true. Thus, she is different from women who leave to have babies, can't think analytically, are not wholly committed to their work, move when their husbands move, refuse to travel because they must look after their families, or won't take a company transfer because their partners won't like it. She does not want to be singled out as a woman because she wants her work and achievements to be valued on their merit. In order to provide this evidence, she must work exceptionally hard herself, but she must also distance herself from other women. In Chase's terms (1988), the career woman firmly resists any form of 'de-professionalisation' by being associated with gender issues. This distancing from other women results in a 'gender-blindness' that is appropriated by the organisation to suit its purposes, and then translated into 'gender-neutrality'. As Kanter (1977: 216) has said:

> The token does not have to work hard to have her presence noticed, but she does have to work hard to have her achievements noticed.

But, as Olsson and Walker (2003) found in their interviews, those very senior women who deny the role of gender in their own career success equally do not want to be perceived as masculinised. This is the classic 'double bind' (e.g. Lakoff 1975; Hochschild 1974), which posits that if women appear to speak and act like other women, they will be deemed too weak to be leaders, and if they speak and sound like men they will be deemed to be aggressive and unwomanly.

Thus women who claim to work successfully in the gender-neutral organisation are constantly 'treading a very fine line'. As Newton (1979) colourfully put it, they must:

> Think like a man, act like a lady, and work like a dog.

The women who have made it to the top and stay there successfully are often extraordinary and outstanding people; they have managed to accomplish a balancing act in their speech and behaviour between being sufficiently professional on one hand and sufficiently feminine on the other (Holmes 2006; Schnurr 2008). This takes great mental agility, linguistic expertise, exceptional energy and hard work. In my experience, this type of gender-neutral identity for a professional woman is likely to be as gender-specific as any other, because the senior women who thrive in male-dominated contexts have learnt that gender-neutrality is one of the best strategies for female success. Gender neutrality is just one of a range of 'gendered discourses' that work to sustain the Male-Dominated corporation in its various guises even in current times.

Gendered discourses

We can see gendered discourses as a more updated, complex and nuanced way of viewing masculinised cultures and leadership-role stereotyping (see above), because discourses, like metaphor, operate subconsciously by pervading people's thoughts, attitudes and beliefs as well as collective cognitions, norms and values (Sunderland 2004).

Brewis (2001: 288) suggests that a dominant discourse is that professional workplaces 'are neutral, non-discriminatory environments in which relations are governed by objectivity and rationality...to ensure that there is no reward for anything other than individual merit'. She adds that gendered discourses, and particularly the 'discourse of gender difference' is of particular relevance to this version of organisational truth. She suggests that it should be seen in connection with a discourse of 'scientific modernism', which work together to promote 'understandings and representations of women as being less suited to organisational life' (2001: 288). In other words, women don't fit the presumed scientific, rational spirit of business life whereas men do!

A discourse of gender difference is the overarching means by which other gendered discourses are reproduced, according to Sunderland (2004). This discourse supports the view that males and females are two quite distinct entities with very little overlap between the two, biologically or culturally. Gender difference attributes polarised qualities to males and females so that *males* are viewed as more rational, independent, competitive and confrontational, while *females* are seen as more irrational, dependent, co-operative, passive, and conciliatory. From a dominance perspective, the male character profile with its more direct, assertive, competitive and confrontational speech style is deemed to be more appropriate for leadership. The female character profile with its more indirect, supportive, hesitant, and collaborative speech style is deemed to be far less appropriate for leadership. In light of this, feminist linguists have argued that 'gender difference' has worked to undermine women at all levels, taking the form of various, quite specific, gendered discourses (Baxter 2003; Brewis 2001; Cameron 2006; Litosseliti 2006; Sunderland 2004).

I shall now consider two of these specific discourses in order to show how they help to perpetuate the view that women are unsuited to leadership in the Male-Dominated corporation.

Discourse of female emotionality/irrationality

This discourse draws on common representations of women as emotional, irrational, intuitive, and caring, and correspondingly, men as rational, unemotional, logical and self-centred. It supports the generalised claim about women using language supportively to connect and to build rapport. The discourse also draws less positively on representations of women as moody, unpredictable and hysterical, which might be manifested linguistically by losing one's temper for no apparent reason, or conversely, using silence to indicate passive aggression.

Litosseliti (2006) draws upon this discourse of emotionality/irrationality and connects it with a discourse of scientific modernism (Brewis 2001) to consider the role of argumentation and debate in business and professional contexts. To this end, she analysed the 'Head to Head' debates in the British newspaper *The Guardian*, which involved a debate between two Chief Executive Officers, the late Anita Roddick of the UK fair-trade cosmetics chain, and Stanley Kalms of Dixons, a UK chain of computer and electrical appliance stores. She shows how Kalms makes a series of attempts to position Roddick's argument symbolically as 'female-as-emotional'. She also shows how Roddick is highly aware of this discourse being used against her, and makes explicit attempts to resist this positioning. In the following extract, the two are discussing the moral duties of business where this discourse is quite explicitly invoked:

> **Kalms:** Anita, our difference may not be so sharp but I can't tell from your scattered thoughts. I believe in a focussed rational approach in which man has it within himself to improve. But it needs a reasoned acceptance of the real world. Might I suggest that Margaret Thatcher would be a better role model than Don Quixote?
>
> **Roddick:** Now I know where you are coming from. I'm the irrational female imposing my world view on my employees, ignorant of how markets work. But you seem to know the price of everything and the value of nothing...
>
> (Litosseliti 2006: 51)

In this extract, Kalms associates himself with 'a focussed rational approach' and 'a reasoned acceptance of the real world' while associating Roddick with random, 'scattered thoughts'. Roddick spots immediately that she is being typecast as 'the irrational female' but tries to make a virtue of this more qualitative view of the world. Litosseliti (2006) concludes in her analysis that there is a 'double discourse' operating in many institutional settings which measures men's and women's achievements by opposing norms. She argues that women's attempts to engage in rational debate are bound to lose out as long as masculinity is associated with rationality and professionalism.

Another case for the influence of the discourse of emotionality/ irrationality in leadership contexts is made by Mullany (2007), who analysed a series of senior management meetings in a retail company and a manufacturing company. She found in her interviews with male middle managers that they would invoke a discourse of 'male as rational' and oppose this with a discourse of 'female as irrational' when asked whether they would prefer to work for a male or a female boss:

> **Martin:** when I did have a female boss they (.) they do tend to be a bit more emotional than men you know I think men can be pretty hard but probably straighter [ ]
>
> **Louise:** [mhm]

Martin: whereas women tend to be (.) I don't know some
women can play (.) the fact that they are a woman and
other women tend to be more emotional...

(Mullany 2007: 186)

Mullany also noted that it wasn't simply men who invoked this discourse, but that female middle managers equally drew upon it as a means of explaining their speech and behaviour:

Amy: I mean Jack I think finds me a complete nightmare (.)
Louise: Really?
Amy: Oh yeah I yeah I mean like I have been so hormonal since I've been here it's untrue I'm the most unemotional person in the world and suddenly I will burst into tears...

(Mullany 2007: 188)

Even though women are complicit in perpetuating this discourse of irrationality, Mullany argues that it is hugely negative and damaging to females because it reinforces the sense that they are inappropriately placed in the workplace and therefore unfit for leadership positions.

Discourse of femininity: image and sexuality

In line with the discourse of emotionality/irrationality is that of an associated discourse of femininity centring on the female image and sexuality. Sinclair (1998) argues that femininity remains a pejorative term amongst most managers, both male and female, because it conveys the opposite of leadership. If there is one thing that has united feminists and liberal female managers, she suggests, it is the desire to avoid the label 'feminine' because it simultaneously defines a woman as more frivolous and therefore, ineffective.

According to Sinclair (1998), a strong sense of sexual identity can be a liability for women in leadership roles. Attractiveness tends to increase the chance of a woman being stereotyped as a sex object or a 'Seductress'. Gutek and Morasch (1982) use the concept of the 'sex-role spill-over' to show that when there are one or two women among men (as is commonly the case in senior management roles) the sex of the woman, rather than other attributes, becomes salient.

As I discussed on gender neutrality, women in Male-Dominated corporations have to work to establish leadership by uncoupling their sexual identity from their leadership persona or minimising the salience of their sex.

Sinclair (1998) analyses how power and femininity are in a constant state of tension within a discourse of image and sexuality, determining a range of semiotic (signifying) systems such as speech styles, dress and appearance and sexual display (Kress and Leeuwen 1996). She identifies four types of female leaders in terms of how they negotiate their power and femininity as shown in Figure 2.3:

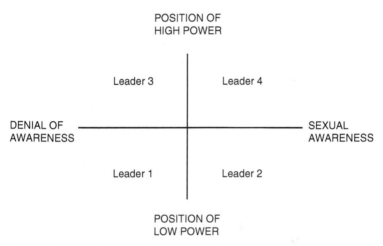

Figure 2.3 A model of sexuality and power for women

According to Sinclair's tabulation above, the quadrants determine the speech and behaviour of four types of female leaders in the following ways (I have added comments on the implications for a leader's *speech* style, which Sinclair does not address):

Leader 1: Denial of sexuality/low power: this type of leader is exhibited by dressing in disguise. One senior woman advises others to 'play down your sexuality and "dowdify" yourself. I wore expensive suits in black, navy and grey, which I have now buried' (cited in Sinclair 1998). The linguistic version of this for a female leader would be to use a language of powerlessness and deficiency (Lakoff 1975): very polite, correct, respectful, indirect, and under-emphatic.

Leader 2:   *High sexual awareness/low power:* this type of leader is exhibited by a highly feminine if groomed appearance. At senior level, women would be expected to be the confidants of men and may be subject to constant, low-level, flirtation if not sexual harassment. Linguistically, women would again use polite, indirect language, (Lakoff 1975) or at best conform to a feminine speech style (Coates 2004): co-operative, supportive, caring and involved.

Leader 3:   *Denial of sexuality/high power:* this type of leader advocates the 'gender-neutral' stance where women seek to play down their femininity and play up their abilities on the basis of their hard work and achievements in the company. The linguistic correlative of this would be to avoid seeming either too stereotypically feminine or too masculine – the classic female double bind (Lakoff 1975).

Leader 4:   *High sexual awareness/high power:* this type is presented as Sinclair's (1998) solution to the 'problem' of women at senior level. Sinclair offers a number of controversial strategies for aligning power with sexuality: exploiting the special sense of being a woman among men; being attracted to people at work and showing it; being confident and in control; looking good physically and displaying femininity prominently; making the most of networks with other women. Linguistically, female leaders would utilise a wide repertoire of speech strategies stereotypically coded male and female. This linguistic approach is explored fully in Chapter 4 where it would be deemed appropriate within a Gender-Multiple corporation. However a stance of high sexual awareness/ high power would be difficult for a female leader to achieve within a Male-Dominated corporation where gender transgression would be judged quite harshly.

What Sinclair's analysis does *not* address is the role of gendered discourses in terms of how they work constantly to mediate an individual leader's sense of agency and experience of reality. Gendered discourses seek to position people in ways that they can not always fully control and may be unable to resist, and that is why female leaders need to be linguistically aware of the power of discourses to shape organisational norms and values.

Mullany (2004) argues that gendered discourses are often 'hegemonic', and they permeate attitudes, male and female, to a crippling degree. She takes the case of Carrie, a Managing Director of a manufacturing company as an example of an extraordinary female leader who in many ways exhibits Sinclair's characteristics for a senior woman who has high power and high sexuality. She shows how David, a middle manager and one of her subordinates, objects to Carrie because she uses her 'gender' to unduly influence men in the business. While this man has said that he likes to look at attractive women in the company, he is unable to reconcile this with women who may be 'using' their sexuality to wield greater power and influence. In his interview with Mullany (2004: 200), he draws on a discourse of sexuality that routinely associates women with devious and manipulative speech and behaviour. Talking of another colleague, Sharon, who is the same rank as him, he says:

David: I have no doubt in my mind that she used her sexual (.) erm wiles if that's the right

Louise: [mm]

David: word [laughs] er you know (.) to get what she wanted in the business

Here, David's reference to the mythologised stereotype that women are prepared to use their sexuality to gain advantages at work also signifies their apparent unsuitability for leadership roles, not least because they distract men from their otherwise honourable endeavour!

Thus, gendered discourses that operate more broadly in western culture can never be sealed off from the workplace and will always influence and mediate people's views. In the Male-Dominated corporation, they serve to reinforce prejudices against women as leaders, and can be deeply undermining. In the examples I have discussed above, gendered discourses have the effect of limiting and harming the way women are evaluated and represented, and perhaps being perceived as potential role models by junior colleagues.

The next two chapters will explore ways in which such discourses can be contested within different types of corporation, in order to broaden and change the range of ways in which women leaders are perceived and judged. Within less traditional types of corporation – the Gender-Divided or the Gender-Multiple, such discourses can be more easily challenged and overturned. These other types of corporation offer greater institutional support and opportunity for female leadership success, as we will now see.

3
Speaking in the Gender-Divided Corporation

> Men are from Mars and Women are from Venus.
>
> (John Gray 1992)

> Men and women are different. Not better or worse – different. Just about the only thing they have in common is that they belong to the same species. They live in different worlds with different values and according to quite different rules.
>
> (Pease and Pease 2001)

You may initially feel that the Gender-Divided corporation, based on the principle of gender difference, is barely a step forward from the Male-Dominated corporation described in the last chapter. Once again, many organisations today might deny that gender difference affects the distribution of jobs, individual career progress, conditions of work or pay – especially in light of legislation and professional codes of practice that seek to guarantee gender equality. Yet in my research experience, many companies in the western world have elements within them of gender difference, even if these are usually experienced quite subtly through attitudes, terms of address, speech styles, behaviour, appearance, dress and 'representations' of people in internal communications. Traditional as it still may be, the Gender-Divided corporation is definitely a better place to work for senior women than the Male-Dominated version in the sense that women are generally valued and supported rather than marginalised or disparaged.

As before, the chapter first describes the theoretical basis of the Gender-Divided corporation from a 'gender difference' perspective, in order to characterise its strengths and weaknesses as a work environment for senior women. Secondly, I explore the features of this type of linguistic environment in order to assess its implications for enabling and/or hindering effective female leadership.

The Gender-Divided corporation

So what are the features of the classic Gender-Divided corporation? This type of organisation is based on the view that men and women have fundamentally different natures and characteristics, just as if they have come from different planets (Gray 1992, 2002). This is reflected quite simplistically in their speech styles where men are expected to be more assertive, direct, confrontational and competitive, while women are expected to be more indirect, supportive, co-operative and facilitative. Males and females adopt different roles in the organisation: males tend to dominate at senior management levels, females at middle or lower management level, although there are token women at the very top to take on the caring and training roles such as Human Resources and Corporate Responsibility. Women are therefore appreciated for the roles they fulfil, but may find it difficult to gain access to all corporate roles. Women in the organisation are in touch with the feminine aspects of their leadership styles and believe that this makes a significant contribution to the organisation.

This chapter explores business and management contexts in which male and female managers show evidence of using language differently and considers what implications this has for leadership. However, unlike the previous chapter, the use of a gender-divided language does not always imply that these are male-dominated contexts. Rather, the prevailing view in the Gender-Divided corporation is that males and females are equal: they use two rather different versions of the language of leadership, but each version is positively evaluated for its complementary strengths. However, this is not a benign state of affairs. While the Gender-Divided corporation can value the supposed attributes, skills and experiences of women very highly, it has a tendency to *generalise* about what females can and can't do, which imposes limitations on their expected range of speech, behaviour and effectiveness as leaders. Polarising male and female speech styles can lead to stereotyping which is limiting for both women and men. However, women get the worse deal as the corporation traditionally favours masculine qualities over feminine.

Popular literature

Over the past couple of decades, countless self-help and popular psychology books have been published portraying men and women as different species and conversation between them as a catalogue of misunderstandings (Cameron 2007). This 'difference' between the sexes has been linked to the high divorce rate in western countries, and to problems of miscommunication between male and female colleagues in the workplace. Advice on how to bridge the communication gap between the sexes has become a multi-million pound industry. John Gray's official website, for example, promotes not only his 'Mars and Venus' books but also seminars, residential retreats, a telephone helpline and a dating service. The feminist linguist, Deborah Tannen (1990, 1994b), has also become an international bestselling author by transforming dry academic research studies into jaunty tales of everyday conversations between men and women. The thesis of Pease and Pease (2001), offering to explain 'why men don't listen and women can't read maps' is also reflected in many contemporary management books and workplace communication training materials.

The appeal of such popular literature does suggest that there might be some 'truth' in the explanation that males and females use the same language in rather different ways. Much of it refers to popular discourses on genetic 'brain-sex' differences, explaining that the gulf between males and females is a product of nature rather than nurture. According to this view (Kimura 1999; Pinker 2002) the sexes communicate differently (and females do it better) because of the way their brains are wired. As a result of 'language lateralisation', the female brain excels in verbal tasks whereas the male brain is better adapted to visual-spatial and mathematics tasks. This genetic difference is used to account for the perception that women like to talk, but men prefer action. It helps to support and reaffirm popular stereotypes of males and females with clichés such as 'women talk too much', 'men don't listen', 'men are more decisive' and 'women get hysterical'. The 'gender as biological difference' approach of these books clearly appeals to many people's common sense way of explaining and dealing with the gender differences and inequalities they see around them on a daily basis. The problem is that presumed gender differences in communication styles and patterns of conversation can play a major role in reinforcing men and women's prejudices and stereotypes of whether or not women are capable of being effective leaders.

This chapter considers the research evidence in support of gender differences in communication style, both in the field of language and gender, and in business and management literature in order to assess whether there is indeed 'a language of female leadership' – one of the two key aims of this book. I look at two major perspectives: the 'deficiency' and the 'difference' perspectives. While I question the idea that there are inherent or even *socialised* differences between male and female speakers, I argue that a *discourse* of gender difference does indeed influence the workings of many corporate cultures. This discourse produces particular versions of reality that value and continually reproduce separate feminine and masculine ways of speaking at leadership level. These may have significant implications for women's effectiveness at leadership level, which are unlikely to be in the best interests of female executives in the longer term.

'A woman's language'

> Men will with great justice object that there is a danger of the language becoming languid and insipid if we are always to content ourselves with women's expressions, and that vigour and vividness count for something. ...Woman as a rule follows the main road of language, where man is often inclined to turn aside into a narrow footpath or even to strike out a new path for himself.
>
> (Otto Jesperson 1922: 215)

This early 20th century view of how women use language is described as the 'deficiency perspective' because it considers that females use a deficient or inferior version of the language spoken by men. The views of Professor Otto Jesperson are arguably those of an old-fashioned misogynist, at best shaped by the historical conditions of the time. However, his deficiency perspective was later taken on by the famous US feminist linguist, Robin Lakoff (1975), who felt that American women were socialised into a quite different way of speaking than men. She argued that women are expected from an early age to 'speak like a lady': to be more conservative of expression, polite, indirect and refined than men. According to Lakoff (*ibid*), this added up to a different and distinct 'women's language': a less confident, uncertain, more powerless version of male language, and consequently, inferior (see Figure 3.1). In her view, this led to the classic 'double bind':

> ...a girl is damned if she does and damned if she doesn't. If she refuses to talk like a lady, she is ridiculed and subjected to criticism as unfeminine. If she does learn [ladylike language], she is ridiculed as unable to think clearly, unable to take part in a serious discussion: in some sense as less than fully human. These two choices which a woman has – to be less than a woman, or less than a person – are highly painful.
>
> (Lakoff, 1975)

The reason that it is important to recall Lakoff's (*ibid*) deficiency theory of female language, is that not only is the double bind still very much with us today (see Chapter 5), but that it had an important effect on the language of a generation of women in the business world. The notion of a deficient woman's language was widely held in the 1970s and led to a movement in following decades to train women managers to be more *assertive*: in short, to stand up for themselves. Assertiveness training (AT) focused on particular strategies for communicating verbally in order to encourage 'clear, honest and direct communication' (cited in Cameron 1995: 176). This exhorted trainees to practise, for example, making 'I' statements such as:

> 'I feel unhappy when I am asked to take the Minutes',
> Or: 'I disagree with you because....'

AT was taken up by feminist business women at the time because it was felt that female socialisation discouraged such assertive traits as directness, willingness to challenge others and to express your own feelings and needs, while on the other hand it encouraged women o   Lexical hedges or fillers, e.g. *you know, sort of, well, actually, you see*

o   Tag questions, e.g. *she's very nice, isn't she?*

o   Rising intonation on declaratives, e.g. *it's really good?*

o   'Empty' adjectives, e.g. *wonderful, lovely, charming, cute, nice, super*

o   Precise colour terms, e.g. *magenta, aquamarine, mauve, taupe*

o   Intensifiers such as *really, so, totally*, e.g. *'It was so nice to meet you'*

o   Mitigating expressions: *just, sort of, perhaps, maybe, kind of, like, a little bit*

o   Hypercorrect grammar, e.g. *consistent use of standard verb forms*

o   'Super-polite' forms, e.g. indirect requests: *Won't you please take a seat*

o   Euphemisms and understatement: e.g. *he passed away; that wasn't very nice*

o   Avoidance of strong swear words, e.g. *bother, my goodness, oh dear, oh my god*

o   Emphatic stress, e.g. *'It was a BRILLIANT performance.'*

o   Apologies: e.g. *I'm so sorry that...*

Figure 3.1   Features of women's language that were considered to be 'deficient'
Source: Lakoff 1975; adapted from Holmes 2001

to resort to indirect, manipulative and underhand strategies. Although AT was later rejected by the business world as a movement that encouraged women to speak like men (Cameron 1995), its aims were to invite women (and some men) to find a place on the assertiveness spectrum between sounding overly tentative on one hand and overly aggressive on the other. Arguably, this kind of approach has since been institutionalised within mainstream management training programmes. Some might say that the longer term influence of AT on today's female leaders has been almost too successful; the spectre of the Iron Maiden or the 'bully broad' are too prevalent in some boardrooms. However, I suggest that most senior women are highly attuned to their position on the assertiveness spectrum, judging carefully when it should be used and when it should be moderated (see Chapter 5).

To professional people today, the perception that women's language is a different and deficient version of men's may now seem a distant memory. Yet, in my experience, this proposition still resonates with many women in professional contexts. I clearly remember that as a teacher educator in charge of groups of trainee English teachers, my communication style was described by a male govern-ment inspector as 'tentative', while my male colleague's style was described as 'charismatic', yet we had both received top ratings from our student groups! Indeed, eminent scholars in business and man-agement studies continue to conceptualise the female speech style as deficient. For example, Still (2006) suggests that 'women need to learn leadership speak'. She adds:

> Although feminists and other progressives may object to this strategy, believing it to devalue women's skills, capabilities and uniqueness, it is a cultural fact that the vast majority of the work-place expects 'leadership speak' from their leaders. Leadership itself demands a certain language and linguistic style – just listen to any politician or business leader!
>
> (Still 2006: 189)

In 'glass ceiling' literature, Powell (2000) argues that at the indi-vidual level, women still lack the necessary qualities such as ambi-tion and confidence in comparison to men as well as leadership skills such as assertiveness and influencing behaviour, and they need to acquire these. So it seems that, after all, this view is still very much with us!

However, many other scholars in the field have taken the oppos-ing view that the feminine speech style is not only *more* suited to the business world but represents the *future* language of leadership for both males and females. The next section introduces the 'gender difference' theory in order to consider this claim, and also to assess whether this theory can inform our understanding of what consti-tutes a language of *female* leadership and possibly, a language of *effective* leadership.

Gender difference theory

Different goals

The main problem with the deficiency perspective is that it takes an 'androcentric' or male-as-norm view of women's language: it tends to *agree* with the assumption that male speech is superior to female speech, and that women should alter their speech to sound more like men. Difference theory has contested the deficiency stance in terms of its failure to engage with female conversational goals, which may be quite different but equally valid as male goals. Women are speaking differently for good reason!

So, a key principle of difference theory is that the language of males and females, as signified by their speech styles, is different but *equal:* it is geared towards achieving different but equally important ends. Support for such a distinction has come from various sources: for example, psychologically-oriented research on gender difference (Gilligan 1989), and gender differences in epistemological development (Belenky, Clinchy, Goldberger and Tarule 1988), both of which characterise the feminine orientation as focusing on relationship and connection, and the masculine orientation as focusing on self and separateness. Difference theory supports the idea of sex-role socialisation; that is, males and females have been socialised into different sub-cultures to have different expectations and requirements of their lives. According to intercultural theorists Maltz and Borker (1982), this difference affects the way people learn to speak. As children, males and females often play and socialise in single-sex social groupings which operate according to different conversational goals. They argue that the primary life goal of *females* is to connect and engage with others, which means that their speech is used to achieve three major outcomes:

- To build relationships of equality and trust
- To co-operate with others to get things done
- To express feelings and emotions

(Maltz and Borker 1982: 20)

These outcomes are achieved by a gendered speech style which is said to be personal, indirect, co-operative, expressive and supportive (see Figure 3.2).

According to this world-view, a strong concern for females is to avoid confronting people, especially other women, in a direct and aggressive way. But this does not mean that women don't actually feel as much aggression or competitiveness as men, according to the authors. Females feel the same way as males in many contexts, but they have been *socialised* to disguise it. Maltz and Borker (*ibid*) suggest that because females tend to avoid showing aggression with each other directly, their more negative emotions tend to 'go under-

Personal:	confessional
	expressive of feelings
	anecdotal
	mirroring of experiences
	self-disclosure: hedges and fillers, pauses and hesitations
Compliant:	use of mitigated directives (avoidance of confrontation)
	e.g. *let's use these first; shall we take turns?*
	facilitative tag questions, e.g. *you would like to go, wouldn't you?*
	minimal responses, e.g. *uh huh, mhm, OK*
	hedges and fillers, e.g. *I mean, perhaps, actually, like you know, sort of*
	qualifying expressions, e.g. *I think that, I feel, in my view, perhaps*
Polite:	a lack of swearing or terms of abuse
	compliments
	terms of endearment
Co-operative:	listening: nods, eye contact
	minimal responses
	overlaps; simultaneous or jointly produced talk
	personal and inclusive pronouns:
	tag questions/asking questions
	eye contact, smiling and head nodding
	mirroring listener's actions
	agreeing;
	acknowledging the previous speaker
Process-orientated:	scene setting
	use of open-ended questions
	hypothesising
	speculating
	egalitarian decision-making
	jointly negotiated leadership

Figure 3.2 Speech features associated with a female speech style

ground', and are either manifested as passive aggression or as meanness and 'bitchiness'. This proposition was explored quite brilliantly in the film *Mean Girls* (Paramount Pictures 2004) in which the lead character, played by Lindsay Lohan, arrives as a fresh innocent from Africa to discover that girls in American High Schools act in strange, savage and manipulative ways. She learns that, just like the boys, girls do operate in hierarchies, they vie to be 'Queen Bee', and they negotiate their female relationships 'behind each other's backs' through an unpleasant concoction of back-stabbing, bitching and trickery. Once a girl attains the status of 'Queen Bee', she has to carefully negotiate this role with her friends so that she is not seen to be 'bossy'. In the film, 'bossiness' or ordering other females around is not regarded as legitimate because it denies equality among women. In a climactic scene at the end of the film, a feminist teacher (accused of being a 'lesbian' by her students) encourages all the senior girls in the school to' talk out' their long-held animosities. Speaking out in public, more stereotypically associated with males, is seen to have huge healing effects in this school community (Baxter 2006c).

In line with the film, difference theorists have shown that much adult speech behaviour begins in childhood and develops during adolescence. Goodwin (1998) in her classic U.S. study of children's subcultures suggests that *girls* learn to direct things without seeming bossy, or they learn not to direct at all. For example, girls will 'mitigate' or soften the orders and commands they make to their friends, as in the following examples where they are using modal auxiliary verbs (e.g. 'could') and hedges (e.g. 'maybe') to organise a game:

Pam: We <u>could</u> go around looking for bottles. (*Modal verb*)
Sharon: Hey <u>maybe</u> tomorrow we <u>can</u> come up here and see if
         they got some more. (*Hedge; modal verb*)

While disputes are as common among girls as they are among boys, girls learn to phrase their arguments in terms of group needs and situational requirements rather than in terms of personal power, desire or animosity. The carefully mediated ways in which *female leaders* have learnt to assert authority will be investigated in detail in Chapters 5 and 6, but in some cases they use rather similar methods to the girls above!

In contrast, the primary life goals of males according to Maltz and Borker (1982) is to compete with other males in order to enhance their authority, and to impress both males and females. Accordingly males tend to use speech in the following three major ways:

• To compete with others for access to 'the floor'
• To use referential, goal-orientated language
• To say things for impact and effect.

(Maltz and Borker 1982: 207)

These goals are achieved by a gendered speech style which is described as competitive, adversarial, controlling, display and task-driven (see Figure 3.3).

Matter of fact:	informative; factual, transactional, referential
	avoidance of emotion and self-disclosure
	discourse markers, e.g. *right, OK, so, now,*
	sequential, taking orderly turns
Assertive:	use of imperatives
	'aggravated' directives; *Give me the pliers; Get off my steps*
	interruptions
	use of declaratives
	challenging, arguing, confronting
	controlling topics
	monologues
Aggressive:	fewer compliments;
	swearing and taboo;
	insults; threats; name-calling
	finger-pointing; fist shaking
	verbs of action, force, violence
Use of humour:	jokes, puns, witticisms, shaggy dog stories, mick-taking, mocking, jeering
Ego-enhancing:	boasting,
	name-dropping
	references to who-you-know, what you've done
Goal-directed:	'what's the answer?'
	'let's get on with it'
	'this is how to solve it'
	taking over; taking control
	clear, single-person leadership
	hierarchical decision-making

Figure 3.3   Speech features associated with a male speech style

A strong concern for males is to gain access to the 'conversational floor', and once there, to maintain it. This is connected with the need for power – to assert authority over peers and subordinates in order to gain a dominant position within the social hierarchy – and also to display that power in ways that draw attention to it. Males achieve this in various ways, according to Coates (2004). She suggests that monologues (where one person speaks at length without interruption) allow males to 'play the expert', which she describes as a 'conversational game where participants take it in turns to hold the floor and to talk about a subject on which they are an expert' (Coates 2004: 134). Other ways for males to achieve their goals are by verbal sparring (an exchange of rapid-fire comments to display wit or intellect); by interruptions in order to take over the floor from another speaker; or by giving orders and commands in direct and unmitigated ways.

According to Coates (2004), asserting authority through the use of commands, orders and instructions is generally far less of a problem for males than it is for females, because males are culturally *expected* to do this, so they are less likely to incur resentment as women might do. A male leader is far less likely to be described as 'bossy' or 'scary' for delivering an order rather too sharply than a female leader is. This was illustrated in Goodwin's (1998) study of US children's sub-cultures, which discovered that alpha male boys are prepared to deliver orders and instructions in 'aggravated' rather than mitigated ways:

Michael: <u>Gimme</u> the pliers (*Poochie gives pliers to Michael*)
Huey: <u>Get off</u> my steps (*Poochie moves down the steps*)

These orders are often supported with statements of desires:

Michael: Gimme the wire...look man, I want the wire cutters right now

However, what might be deemed acceptable in child's play, that is, a no-nonsense approach to telling others what to do, is not necessarily regarded as sophisticated or appropriate at adult or leadership level. As leaders today look for diverse and flexible strategies to deal with complex and competing business goals, the traditional 'command and control' style of management is increasingly regarded as irrelevant. I am one of a number of commentators (Baxter 2008) who has noted a more 'feminised' leadership speech style used by both men and women in many current business environments. Given that the feminine way of 'doing leadership' may be more highly regarded, I shall consider this possible 'appropriation' by male leaders in Chapter 4.

Popular and academic theorists alike (e.g. Coates 2004; Gray 2002) have argued that one consequence of identifying gendered speech styles is that these can lead to miscommunication between the sexes.

They suggest that such miscommunication has implications for managing relationships between male and female leaders in the workplace.

Miscommunication

If women and men have contrasting cultural *rules* for conversations, such rules may come into conflict when women and men attempt to talk to each other as equals. According to difference theorists (Coates 2004; Maltz and Borker 1982; Tannen 1994a), males and females often use the same speech features in different ways which is a recipe for misunderstanding as shown in Figure 3.4:

Use of questions: there are two interpretations of the meanings of questions. Women tend to use questions as part of conversational maintenance, whereas men tend to see questions as requests for information.

Example: a woman may ask a man a question to stimulate small talk, but a man may answer it lengthily and seriously, assuming that the woman wants a 'real' answer!

Use of minimal responses (uh huh, yeah, OK): women tend to use these to show that they are listening to the speaker and showing support for a conversational topic. Men tend to use them to agree with a point.

Example: a man may feel that a woman is agreeing with everything he is saying, whereas the woman may be merely showing interest and encouraging him to continue speaking.

Problem-sharing and advice-giving: women tend to discuss problems with each other, sharing experiences and giving reassurances, Men in contrast tend to hear women and other men who present them with problems as making explicit requests for solutions. They respond by giving advice, acting as experts and lecturing to their audiences.

Example: a woman may find that when she discusses a problem with a man, he jumps to providing a solution, rather than just providing a sympathetic ear.

Verbal aggressiveness: whereas women seem to interpret overt aggressiveness as personally directed, negative and disruptive, men seem to view it as merely a means of organising conversational flow, as in the form of an argument or a debate.

Example: a woman may find that because a man disagrees with her argument he is also attacking her. A woman, in avoiding aggression, may be taken less seriously as a debating partner, but here the 'double bind' kicks in. If she appears verbally assertive, she may be disparaged as 'an aggressive woman'.

(based on Maltz and Borker 1982: 213)

Figure 3.4   Speech features causing miscommunication between males and females

While various self-help guides and workshop manuals offer advice directed primarily at women to help them overcome miscommunication with men (e.g. Gray 2002; Pease and Pease 2001), there is really only anecdotal evidence to back up such advice. However, the extraordinary popularity of the 'Mars and Venus' phenomenon suggests that many people round the world feel that there is a link between gendered speech styles and miscommunication!

In the next two sections, I examine the nature of the research evidence for gender-differentiated speech styles in order to assess the value of difference theory for understanding what constitutes the language of female leadership. In the first section, I consider three classic research studies from the field of language and gender (Holmes 1992; Kendall 2006; West 1998), and in the subsequent section, I review three difference-based studies from the field of leadership and organisational behaviour.

The language and gender perspective

According to Tannen (1994), male speakers are socialised into a competitive or 'report' style of interaction, whereas female speakers are socialised into a co-operative or 'rapport' style of interaction. All three of the following studies seem to support that claim. First, in Candace West's (1984/1998) study of doctor-patient relationships, she discovered that women and men doctors issue directives in very different ways. In line with Goodwin's (1998) research on children using directives, West showed that women doctors were more likely than men to use directive forms which elicit a compliant response from the patient. Male doctors preferred to use imperative forms or statements in which they *told* patients what they 'needed' to do, or what they 'had' to do. Women doctors on the other hand, often constructed directives in the form of proposals for joint action as these examples illustrate:

(1) Okay! Well let's make that our plan!
(2) So let's stay on uh what we are doing right now OK?

This use of proposals for joint action is similar to strategies used by female leaders in business contexts, which I examine in Chapter 6.

Secondly, and more closely relevant to business leadership, Janet Holmes (1992) found key gender differences between the way senior men and women participated in meetings. She looked at the different ways in which males and females took part in 100 public meetings and seminars, particularly focusing on the access of both sexes to 'public space' during question times. She found that men dominated the question time, asking 75% of the questions, although she notes that 'this was not surprising' as there were more men present on these occasions (Holmes 1992: 133). But even in sessions where there were *equal* numbers of males and females, men asked 62% of all the questions in all but seven of the 100 sessions. This gap in terms of the number of contributions made in a question-answer session is reinforced by my own case study (Chapter 6) in which I found that female managers who were participants in meetings, made far fewer contributions than male managers who were participants.

Holmes' (1992) study also found *qualitative* differences in the ways in which males and females participated in these meetings. She identified three types of elicitations (questions put to the speaker or Chair) as 'supportive', 'critical' and 'antagonistic', and found that men were twice as likely as women to use 'antagonistic elicitations' ('challenging, aggressively critical assertions whose functions were to attack the speaker's position and demonstrate it as wrong'). Below, example (3) is an antagonistic elicitation spoken by a male participant, whereas (4) is a supportive elicitation spoken by a female participant:

(3) I have to say I disagree with your analysis. The elements you have identified as important seem relatively insignificant to me compared to the crucial influence of...

(4) I really liked your comments on...could you expand a little on the Thai data? What do you think is going on in Table 2?
                                                                    (Holmes 1992: 138)

Holmes suggests that there are two kinds of talk considered to be powerful or influential in public meeting settings. The first she termed 'valued talk' used more by men, which is likely to be status-enhancing in that effective public speaking earns respect in public contexts. The second she named 'valuable talk' used more by women, which is likely to be more socially connecting and cognitively stretching. Holmes

(1992: 135) argues that this latter type of talk, used more by women than men and distinguished by supportive and critical elicitations, is vital to 'improve the quality of [any] discussion', but doesn't always receive public recognition.

Thirdly, Shari Kendall's (2006) work on business and managerial contexts suggests that there are gender differences in the ways in which female and male managers handle authority. In her study of managerial behaviour at a national radio network station, she noticed that while Carol, a technical director, tended to downplay her authority in order to support Ron, her co-director, Ron spoke in such a way that enhanced his own authority and undercut Carol's. Kendall (2006) shows how Carol lowered her voice and used hedges to 'mitigate' (soften) her suggestions so as not to threaten Ron when she disagreed with him about the need for a 'back-up' plan:

> **Carol:** All right. I've got a call to Andy and uh I'm going to pursue (.) mildly pursue the double (.) double back-up in case.

However, when Ron spoke, he tended to undercut Carol's authority by raising his voice, and repeatedly questioning her about information she had already given him:

> **Ron:** But that's <u>all</u> you know that it was ordered (.) and you <u>did</u> tell the phone company that we had an Adtran?
> **Carol:** Yes I did.

Kendall's point here is that female leaders are more concerned to maintain good 'relational practices' (Fletcher 1999) at the expense of maintaining authority whereas male leaders have the exact opposite priority.

We can see that the three studies reviewed above all take a gender difference perspective to make sense of apparent distinctive differences in the ways in which males and females handle authority. However, many such gender difference studies have since been criticised for the highly *selective* nature of the material chosen to illustrate the writer's argument (Bergvall, Bing and Freed 1996). If a language and gender scholar wants to find evidence of gender difference in speech styles, it is surely going to occur somewhere in a corpus of data. More recent language and gender research has attempted to be more balanced by searching for evidence of *similarities* as well as differences in style (e.g. Baxter 2003). As we will see in the next chapter, more 'rounded' approaches to data gathering and analysis have led to more nuanced conclusions about the role of gender in defining leadership speech styles.

But the difference approach is still deeply entrenched in our way of looking at the world. It is no surprise therefore that gender and leadership theorists have tended to adopt a 'difference' perspective to explaining female and male leadership language, as we shall now see.

The leadership perspective

Two genders, two leadership styles

The 'difference' perspective of language and gender theory above finds an interesting parallel in work conducted by scholars in gender and leadership (e.g. Eagly and Johnson 1990; Korabik 1990; Sealy and Singh 2008; Singh 2002).

Until relatively recently, much of this research adopted a 'person-centred' perspective (see Singh 2007; Terjesen and Singh 2008), which identifies the under-representation of women in senior management as partially a result of gendered differences in traits, aptitudes and behaviours, as well as a result of their interactive style.

Much of this 'person-centred' research with a focus on gender drew its sustenance from early theories of leadership style (e.g. Bales 1951; 1958), which were originally developed through experimental studies conducted in the laboratory using groups of male undergraduates. Bales (1958) found that there are two types of leadership styles:

- A *task-orientated* expert who was concerned with instrumental functions related to the achievement of group goals
- A *socio-emotional* expert whose concern was the morale and cohesiveness of the group.

While Bales found that these two roles were independent and usually fulfilled by different people, subsequent research has demonstrated that a single person frequently does perform both roles as I explore in Chapter 4. But Bales conceived of the two leadership roles as complementary and saw both as necessary for the smooth functioning of the group. Building on Bales' work (*ibid*), scholars first took an interest in the correlation of leadership style with gender, in a range of studies taking place in mixed sex settings ranging from marriage to the courtroom (e.g. Lockheed and Hall 1976; Strodtbeck and Mann 1956). These generally found that males displayed a more task-orientated style and females a more socio-emotional style than males. Furthermore, men and women were evaluated more favourably by subordinates when they conformed to stereotyped roles than when they deviated from them (Petty and Miles 1976). Subsequently, a number of laboratory-based studies (e.g. Eagly and Johnson 1990; Eskilon and Wiley 1976) have shown that in *single-sex* groups, males and females use *both* types of leadership expertise without fear or favour. In short, these studies suggested that there were *no* obvious differences between male and female leadership styles. It was only when males and females were placed in *mixed-sex* groups that males gravitated towards the more task-orientated approach to leadership tasks, whereas females gravitated towards the more socio-emotional approaches. There have been various explanations for this, but Korabik (1990) argues that notions of gender-role socialisation – that males are *expected* to take the lead in mixed-sex settings whilst females are supposed to support and agree – may explain why the different genders often conform to stereotype.

Indeed, Korabik argued that scholars should separate the notion of a person's 'sex' from the cultural construct of their 'gendered' interactional style on the basis that certain people, regardless of their biological sex, were drawn to the 'task-orientated style' while other people were drawn to the 'socio-emotional' style. In laboratory studies Korabik (1982) further demonstrated that 'masculine' individuals of both sexes preferred the 'task-orientated' role, and that 'feminine' individuals of both sexes preferred the 'socio-emotional' leadership role. Her studies gave substantial weight to the view that the cultural construct of gender is a much more powerful criterion in determining the choice of styles of leadership than a person's actual biological sex.

Despite the lack of evidence for *biological* sex differences in speech and leadership styles, the view that women leaders are 'transformational' and male leaders are 'transactional' has become mythologised in certain quarters of gender and leadership literature (Halford and Leonard 2001; Still 2006; Vinnicombe and Singh 2002). As introduced in Chapter 1, according to this perspective a 'transformational' leader is seen as one who is able to get subordinates to transform their own self-interest into the interest of the group through concern for a broader goal. However, arguably, the term 'transformational' has today developed far broader connotations, and is no longer particularly appropriate for describing the female leadership style *only*. Building on Burns' (1978) work, Bass (1985) developed a transformational leadership theory to suggest that this type of leader seeks for new ways of working, identifies new opportunities versus threats, and tries to get the *status quo* to change the environment, qualities that are clearly not exclusive to women.

Alternatively, Fletcher (1999: 9) argued that a female leader's style is particularly characterised by its 'relational practices': that is, 'creating relational connections with others and meeting basic relational needs without calling attention to these needs themselves'. While Fletcher herself saw 'relational practices' as part of female subordination in the workplace, Holmes (2006) has given the term 'relational' far more positive connotations in line with a gender difference view. In her recent work, Holmes (*ibid*) tends to juxtapose the female 'relational' style with the male 'transactional' style, and I have adopted this more accurate terminology in this book. So, in line with this, a woman's management style is typified as being based on personal respect, mutual trust, regard for the contribution that each team member can bring, and the development of the individual and diverse talent. This is conceptualised in opposition to the traditional 'transactional leader', who views job performance as a series of transactions with subordinates – exchanging rewards for services rendered or punishment for inadequate performance. In line with this, a man's management style is often typified as being reliant on power position and formal authority.

A strong theme in gender and leadership literature is that the feminine interactional/speech style has been considerably *undervalued*, and could play a much more significant role in defining constructs of effective leadership. Rosener (1990) found in an international study of leaders that women are much more likely than men to use power based on personal qualities, work record and contacts rather than power based on organisational position, title and the ability to reward and punish. Her views are clearly drawn from the 'gender difference' perspective that males and females are brought up in different sub-cultures (Maltz and Borker 1982):

> ...women have been expected to be wives, mothers, community volunteers, teachers and nurses. In all these roles, they are supposed to be cooperative, supportive, understanding, gentle and to provide services for others. They are to derive satisfaction and a sense of esteem from helping others including their spouses...this may explain why women today are more likely than men to be interactive leaders' (Rosener 1990: 124).

From her interview data, Rosener developed her noted model of 'interactive leadership', labelled as such because she claimed that female leaders actively work to make their interactions with subordinates positive for everyone involved. In her view, interactive leadership reflects the belief of female leaders 'that allows employees to contribute and to feel powerful and important is a win-win situation – good for the employees and the organisation' (Rosener 1990: 120).

Rosener posits that women leaders' use of 'participative management' involves a number of key linguistic strategies, which significantly encourage motivation and more effective performance from their teams. These strategies are to:

- *Encourage participation:* invite others to have a say in almost every aspect of their work; and create mechanisms that get people to participate such as using a conversational style that sends signals encouraging people to get involved.
- *Share power and information:* solicit information from other people, which encourages a flow of information from employees to 'boss'; also make sure that communication flows in two ways; be open and frank; and hold open strategy sessions.
- *Enhance the self-worth of others:* give others credit and praise for good work; refrain from asserting their own superiority; and compliment people appropriately.

- *Energise others* express enthusiasm about work projects to subordinates; and use an upbeat leadership style to get others
  energised by their work.

(adapted from Rosener 1990: 119–125).

Rosener (1990: 125) argues that this feminine interactive style is
of huge benefit to organisations because there is a greater need in
the business climate for a diversity of leadership styles which have
the 'strength and flexibility to survive in a highly competitive [and]
increasingly diverse economic environment'. Making the economic
argument is of course hugely important to scholars in the field of
gender and leadership who wish to convince business practitioners
of the value of their work (see Terjesen and Singh 2008). Theoretically and ideologically, this argument also represents an attempt to
reverse the equally prevalent and popular 'gender deficiency' perspective described on pp. 54–57 above.

But it is not just gender and leadership scholars who are making
the business case for the revaluation of the 'feminine' interactional
leadership style. In my own interviews with male and female leaders
(Baxter 2008), I found that senior women in particular were advo-
cating the business necessity of a 'relational' approach, which was
strongly associated with females rather than males. Indeed, without
prompting from me, a number of the participants referred to 'feminine' and 'masculine' styles of leadership in order to describe their
experiences. Many of these senior women felt that they were offering something different and new to their corporations both linguistically and as people. One leader, the CEO of a small marketing
company, was positively evangelical about women leaders taking
the business world into the future, suggesting that senior women
today have a 'freedom' to express their emotions and passions in a
way that is still closed to men:

I think the masculine side is a 'has-been' in the business world. I
think the workplace environment is changing. Ultimately you
are talking about a leader of people. You no longer have a job for
life; people have choices, and they would not willingly choose a
confrontational and aggressive environment. People want to go
where they feel they can add value and be in control of their own
destiny. The masculine world is undeniably where we have come

from, but we are in a time of transition. Women have that breadth, we have options with our lives that men still don't have.
(CEO, marketing company)

My interview data showed that female leaders do partly construct their sense of identity in terms of gender difference, and that, because they perceive that they are in a man's world, and because they are often exceptional people, they are able to capitalise on that difference as a strength. They are partially tapping into current media discourses of 'masculinity in crisis', which question the continuing patriarchy of male leadership and deem the future to be female (Baxter 1999). They are also tapping into assumptions about a Gender-Divided corporation where the separate strengths of male and female leaders are appreciated in terms of their distinctive merits.

So we can see that the gender difference perspective is today actively shared by leaders and theorists alike. As if it were a brand new insight, Still recently argued that 'men and women need to appreciate that they have different ways of speaking' and that 'management cultures have not awakened to this fact or acknowledged that the use of words may have different cultural meanings because of different socialisation' (2006: 189).

However, current theory in both language and gender and organisation studies has started to critique the 'difference' perspective on a number of grounds. It is important to be aware of this critique because business leaders are fooling themselves if they buy into the 'difference as strength' argument, powerful as it is. The difference perspective is not going to enable senior women to take part on an equal basis in the boardroom as I now discuss.

Critique of the 'gender difference' perspective

The current critique of the 'difference' paradigm stems from a 'discourse' or social constructionist understanding of gender identities (Baxter 2008; Butler 1990; Crawford 1995; Mullany 2007). This broadly argues that the categories of 'men' and 'women' have been used in sweeping and monolithic ways, and that bald associations of speech (or management) styles with gender are far too simplistic. Discourse theorists have questioned gender difference theory on the following four linguistic and philosophical grounds.

First, language itself is always multi-functional and contextually sensitive. It cannot be reduced to a simple correspondence between the sex/gender of the speaker and their use of a particular language style. To give you an example, Lakoff (1975) suggested that women use tag questions (*you could, couldn't you?*) more often than men, which are supposed to denote uncertainty because they reduce the force of an utterance as in:

Laura: You could get a quote for that work couldn't you?

On one level, the tag question could be read as a sign of this speaker's *un*certainty in that she appears to be seeking reassurance for her question. Of course, the use of the tag can only be understood for its full meaning when it is *heard*, which involves prosodic cues such as rising or falling intonation. If it was spoken with *rising* intonation (an upwards rise of the voice), then it might indeed signal *un*certainty. But if the tag was expressed with *falling* intonation, it might alternatively imply *certainty* and perhaps acquire the force of a command. A language feature like this depends for its use on context. Holmes (1995) discovered that both males and females used tag questions for a wide variety of purposes (certainty, uncertainty, to facilitate others, emphasis, etc). Her study certainly challenged the idea that women only use tag questions in one way – to signal their uncertainty and therefore, powerless social status!

Secondly, the way people use speech may be less dependent on their gender and far more dependent on the 'community of practice' also known as CofPs (Wenger 1998), in which they regularly participate. Eckert and McConnell-Ginet (1998) found that people's speech styles vary considerably according to the norms and values of differing CofPs, such as being with family at home, friends in the pub, or with colleagues in the boardroom. Workplace interactions tend to be strongly embedded in the business and social context of a particular work group, as well as in a wider social and cultural order. Marra, Schnurr and Holmes (2006) in their work on leadership, have identified *CofPs* as gendered rather than individual speech styles. They suggest that some business contexts are 'feminised' and other contexts are 'masculinised'. Building on the CofP notion, Terjesen and Singh (2008) suggest that gender differences must be conceptualised not simply from a 'person-centred' viewpoint, nor even from an organisation or 'situation-centred' viewpoint, but from a 'social-system' or macro-structural viewpoint, because gender differences are institutionalised as common practices at societal level and so infuse daily practices in work settings.

A third criticism levelled against gender difference theory is the philosophical one that it is based on *essentialist* assumptions. Essentialists assume that males and females have a fundamental, distinctive nature (whether biologically determined or produced through socialisation), which is fixed, static and not subject to change. An essentialist stance makes binary assumptions about the male and female character, which polarises and dichotomises people into two opposing sexes. This ignores any similarities between males and females. It also ignores the existence of individuals who are inter-sexed or transsexual. Theorists point out that a gender dichotomy is therefore not an inevitable perception: gender might be seen more realistically as a continuum, which involves some overlapping between the sexes, rather than as two polarised categories (Bergvall, Bing and Freed 1996). As Korabik (1990) shows in her research on androgyny and leadership style, there are men who routinely adopt feminised styles and females who adopt masculinised styles in speech, behaviour and leadership.

According to Talbot (1998) the danger of gender difference theory is that it can lead to over-generalisations about males and females, which in turn produces global categorisations ('all males are...') and sex-role stereotyping ('women tend to get moody'). This potentially offers a cultural mandate to treat males and females in different, unequal or prejudicial ways ('women can't make rational decisions so they don't deserve a place in the boardroom').

Fourthly and finally, discourse theorists have criticised the gender difference perspective for regarding gender as more important than other features (such as age, class, ethnicity, professional status, etc) in the make-up of a person's identity. Bucholtz and Hall (1995) argue that identities are constructed and performed by means of a complex system of intersecting features or 'variables', which differ according to context. Thus, there are contexts where a person's gender becomes salient and other contexts where it does not. For example, in a senior management meeting where there are roughly *equal* numbers of men and women, gender is unlikely to be salient, but where there are only one or two women present, gender will feature more prominently as inevitably, women become more 'visible' (Kanter 1977). This is just as likely to apply to other constituents of a person's identity, such as ethnicity, class and educational background. Scholars of 'discourse theory' thus argue that gender should not be overly highlighted but viewed as just one of a number of key variables within leadership and workplace contexts. But if gender is just one variable, this tends to imply that it is no longer an issue in leadership contexts. This is clearly not the case in the female leadership context as I consider in Chapter 4.

In summary, *discourse* theory promises to offer a much more complex and nuanced view of the significance of gender to leadership language than *difference* theory. This is because the discourse approach doesn't regard gender in essentialist terms as person-centred and unchangeable, but as a feature of identity that is being continuously constructed and reconstructed through a person's speech and actions in a given context or community of practice. According to this view, individuals are also immersed in *discourses* – dominant ways of organising the world – which place expectations on how people should think, speak and interact with others. These discourses variously offer people powerful or powerless subject positions within an organisation. Female leaders can choose to take up these positions, negotiate, challenge, resist and change them. It is therefore important to understand the discourse approach to the language of female leadership because it suggests that current business practices can be *changed* so that senior women can be more effective and powerful in the boardroom.

As we shall see in the next chapter, this can be best demonstrated in the context of the Gender-Multiple corporation.

4
Speaking in the Gender-Multiple Corporation

This chapter proposes that the Gender-Multiple corporation can offer female leaders a more hospitable linguistic environment in which to succeed than the Male-Dominated or Gender-Divided Corporations. Early research evidence suggests that this type of corporation is emergent, it exists sporadically in many organisations today, and that it is part of the change agenda of more forward-looking organisations that seek to enhance the talents of people of different genders, ages, ethnicities, and backgrounds. The chapter provides evidence that not only are *individual* senior women initiating more powerful and influential ways of using language in order to enable their own effectiveness as leaders, but *organisations* are developing inclusive, female-friendly practices with which to support this quest.

The Gender-Multiple corporation

In the Gender-Multiple corporation, gender is an important aspect of people's identities but is not *the* defining feature by which individuals are categorised and judged. Members of this corporation view their identity as the result of a fluid mix of gender, age, education, professional status, ethnicity, language, class, personality and so on. In other words, difference and diversity are essential to the way people see themselves. Female leaders for example, regard their femininity to be multi-dimensional rather than defined solely by 'feminine' attributes or limiting stereotypes. They wish to embrace and incorporate the often contradictory identities or 'selves' in their lives: as leaders, career women, friends of other women, colleagues of men and women, mothers, lovers, wives, partners and daughters. There are flexible definitions of gender and sexuality, so that these aspects of identity are viewed as continua or overlapping categories rather than as binary oppositions. This contrasts with the gender-neutral organisation, which dismisses gender as being relevant at all to business and leadership practices.

According to the gender-multiple perspective, females and males have a considerable commonality of experience, expertise, lifestyles and aspirations. Males may associate themselves with qualities conventionally coded 'feminine', while females may associate themselves with qualities conventionally coded 'masculine'. In postmodern spirit (Lyotard 1984), the boundaries between 'male' and 'female', 'masculine' and 'feminine' have thus become more permeable. Consequently, there isn't a noticeable division of roles by gender in the Gender-Multiple corporation, so that there are relatively equal numbers of men and women at all senior levels and across all the business functions (Baxter 2008; Mullany 2007; Schnurr 2008). There are likely to be men as well as women doing work at administrative and clerical levels. Females are welcome at Board level, mentoring of able women is encouraged, and opportunities for promotion are organised by well established diversity policies and career progression routes. Overall, the organisation is highly responsive to change and development, and accepts that people at all levels will constantly question and challenge 'how things are done'.

Furthermore, people's interactional and speech styles help to reflect and construct the notion of gender multiplicity in the corporation. Both male and female leaders are likely to have a wide verbal repertoire using 'masculine' and 'feminine' speech styles with equal facility according to their changing conversational goals. Senior people are readily able to switch between different types of leadership style – transactional, relational and others – in order to be effective. There is therefore little discernible difference between the speech styles of male and female leaders. This is because they are demonstrating linguistic expertise – they know the power of language and are able to flex it to achieve effective leadership in their organisations. Senior people are aware that 'gendered discourses' pervade their organisation and society generally, which could limit their effectiveness, but they are prepared to make these discourses explicit, and question them openly and critically in different forums. Indeed, senior women may invoke gender difference discourses in a playful and ironic way ('we're going to have a girly night out!'), as they are aware of the cultural power and usefulness of such discourses.

Value of discourse theory

Discourse theory is particularly well placed to explain the principles and workings of the Gender-Multiple corporation. We have seen how theories of gender dominance seemed suited to an explanation of Male-Dominated corporations, and theories of gender difference seem appropriate for Gender-Divided corporations (although both have been critiqued by discourse theory; see Chapter 3 above). My premise is that theories are constitutive: they not only seek to conceptualise and explain different structures, institutional practices, cultures, symbols and ideas but they also contribute to the reproduction and maintenance of discourses. In other words, there are clear reasons why a particular theoretical paradigm helps to explain particular cultural or discourse practices. The discourse approach suggests that organisations are always sustained by historically situated discourses: different ways of knowing or making sense of the world (Foucault 1980), which determine how people speak, interact and influence others.

In order to understand the relevance of the discourse approach for the language of female leadership in the Gender-Multiple corporation, the next section examines this theme under three headings: Discourses in the corporation; Social construction of gender identities; and Communities of Practice (CofPs). All three sections are interconnected in various ways, so I will be reflexive about the connections where they occur.

Discourses in the corporation

Brewis (2001) has argued that discourses are 'sets of ideas, theories, symbols, institutions and practices which underpin and reproduce specific ways of knowing and behaving in the world'. They create 'subject positions' – that is, spaces for individuals to locate themselves within and define themselves through. Discourses are always associated with power relations. Thus, dominant discourses make certain forms of knowledge more important and powerful than other forms of knowledge, so that eventually these become 'regimes of truth' (Foucault 1972), influencing common sense thinking and routine practices. They offer unwritten rules and permissions about how people should speak and behave in particular circumstances with 'punishments', prohibitions and exclusions if people speak or behave inappropriately (Weedon 1997). Such 'rules' are often highly subtle, such as who is/feels included or excluded in particular contexts.

I can give a particular example of this notion of prohibition from my own professional context. It was graduation day, and as a member of academic staff, I was expected to be 'on show', sitting at the back of the stage in the grand hall. While I was waiting for the ceremony to begin, a colleague and I inadvertently entered a common room reserved for the university's senior management – that is, the Chancellor, Vice Chancellor and three pro-vice Chancellors ('PVCs'). As we sat and chatted, the only female PVC entered the room and rather imperiously asked us both, 'What on earth are you doing in here?' She obviously viewed us as 'under-lings', of significantly lower status with no rights to sit in this sanc-tuary. As it happened, my colleague is also a personal friend of this PVC, and when the PVC realised who my colleague was, she quickly changed her register and proceeded to engage her in bright, friendly small talk. Throughout the ensuing conversation, the PVC expressly ignored me. Even though this incident made me feel rather small at the time, it did provide me with some very rich material for later analysis! From the perspective of discourse theory, it was possible to identify a dominant discourse of *status and seniority,* which was at odds with a more informal discourse of *female friendship.* The PVC chose to use her subject position as a high ranking member of the university to exclude us both from this setting, but this was in conflict with her competing position as 'a female friend'. I was rendered doubly powerless in this context by my subject position within *both* discourses because I was neither senior enough, nor a personal friend. My colleague was excluded only by the discourse of *status and seniority,* and the PVC managed this 'discursive site of struggle' by not including me!

The effects of dominant discourses do not necessarily imply a deter-ministic universe whereby less powerful individuals must accept their subject positioning. As people we all have some 'agency': that is, the power to adopt the approved subject position, or to resist and under-mine it. Indeed, less powerful individuals or social groups are often responsible for initiating alternative or resistant discourses, which may go unrecognised in the early stages, but are essential in making challenges to received ways of thinking, and in opening up possibilities for future change (Baxter 2003).

How does discourse theory apply to the language of female leadership? Within organisations that are resistant to change, such as the Male-Dominated or the Gender-Divided corporation, the subject positions made available by dominant discourses require compliance, and those who attempt to resist (such as a senior woman using an assertive speech style) could find that they forfeit support from peers or others. However, within organisations that are responsive to change and development, such as the Gender-Multiple corporation, dominant discourses are more malleable, shifting and open to challenge and change. Senior women are likely to have a much greater stake in decision-making and will feel confident to question and change established practices.

In summary, a discourse approach conceptualises the language of female leadership in the following ways:

- All discourses in an organisation are open to contestation, and participants are neither 'controlled' by dominant discourses nor are they 'rational' individuals who make wholly free choices (Weedon 1997). This 'contested world' places female leaders in a position where they can act and make choices (for example, influence their boss; wield a comparable degree of power to male peers) but where they are also constrained by competing discourses that may favour the interests of other colleagues, their seniors and the organisation.
- Many discourses are institutionally initiated and sustained, and represent the interests of established authority. The dominant discourses of an organisation will partially govern whether a female leader feels accepted and included by her colleagues and supported by those on the level above her, or whether she feels excluded and perhaps, isolated.
- However, organisational discourses rarely position leaders as consistently 'powerless' (Brewis 2001): they offer a range of *multi-faceted* subject positions that can be beneficial to them. Diverse

discourses within the Gender-Multiple corporation allow for people to be powerfully positioned within certain contexts but less powerfully positioned within others. So within a corporation that actively supports a discourse of gender equality, a female leader may be able to disregard her minority status in a board-room full of men. But if there is a competing institutional discourse, for example, valuing 'long service' and she happens to be the most recent addition to the Board, she may feel less powerfully positioned than her longer-serving or more experienced colleagues. Of course, in a gender-multiple setting, newly appointed men are equally likely to feel less influential than more experienced colleagues!

- Gendered discourses define which types of knowledge are seen as important or powerful, and which are unimportant or less powerful. They can reinforce how influential certain sets of gendered assumptions are within an organisation, such as male dominance, gender difference, gender deficiency or gender equality and diversity. In the Gender-Multiple corporation, discourses of gender equality and diversity will compete for influence with more traditional discourses such as gender deficiency or difference, for example. As no single gendered discourse dominates in this corporation, any single way of looking at the issues and challenges in their organisation is always open to contestation and debate.

- Competing or counter-discourses that exist in an organisation can offer alternative versions of social reality (i.e. if a group of individuals within the organisation doesn't accept 'the rules' and decides to resist, then it may initiate counter-discourses). Mullany (2007), in her study of a manufacturing and a retail company, shows how female managers attempted to subvert dominant gendered practices by developing resistant discourses associated with feminism, freedom, equal opportunities and female solidarity. Within these types of relatively traditional organisations, counter discourses can be perceived as deeply threatening to the *status quo*, and are therefore expressed in more 'underground' ways (for example, through the creation of informal networks of women). Within a Gender-Multiple corporation, there is much less need for counter-discourses because alternative discourses about gender are expected, welcomed and explored.

Social construction of gender identities

Women and men are different because language positions us differently. In this view, subjectivity – our sense of selves – is something constructed, not pre-given and our gender identities are not fixed. We take up positions in our enactment of discourse practices so our identities are constructed moment by moment.

(Talbot 1998: 144)

The discourse approach to gender draws on social constructionist theory (Butler 1990; Cameron 1997; Crawford 1995) which suggests that males and females are not born, or even socialised into a pre-fixed gender, but they *become* gendered through their interactions. According to this view, individuals don't *have* a gender, they *do* gender through repeated physical and linguistic interactions. This postmodern perspective argues that males and females do not have an individual essence, character or 'core' (Weedon 1997). There are no intrinsic male or female characteristics, only ones that are brought into being through repeated bodily or linguistic actions. These characteristics are the *effects* we produce by way of particular things we do. Thus, according to Butler (1990), people's identities are *performative*. We learn to 'perform' many aspects of our identity such as being feminine or masculine through:

the repeated stylisation of the body, a set of repeated acts within a rigid regulatory frame which congeal over time to produce the appearance of a substance, of a 'natural kind of being'.

(Butler 1990: 33)

In this way, gender has constantly to be reaffirmed and publicly displayed by repeatedly performing particular acts in accordance with the cultural norms or indeed, dominant discourses, of an institution or social group. Cameron (1997: 49) suggests that language can also be conceptualised as 'a repeated stylisation of the body' in that the masculine and feminine speech styles advocated by the gender difference perspective can be viewed as the 'effects' of routine conversations by people 'who are striving to constitute themselves as "proper" men and women'. Language is therefore not just a medium to convey social life and interactions but is an essential constitutive factor. So particular uses of language become culturally associated with masculinity and femininity; they become 'symbolically gendered' (Freed 1996), rather than being the property or attributes of males and females.

According to the social constructionist perspective, gender can therefore be seen as relational, a process, something that is done, and something that is only conventionally a two-system category (Weatherall 2002). If these are cultural constructs only, they can be challenged and resisted. Gender has the potential to be reconceptualised in terms of multiple roles and positions for men and women. There are a range of ways in which people can speak and act, some of which may be stereotypically coded 'masculine' and others 'feminine', but they are potentially available to all. The implication of this for female leaders in the Gender-Multiple corporation is that it may free women from the obligation always to be feminine, to speak and sound like a woman, just as it frees men from the obligation to be masculine, to speak and sound like a man. Preliminary research has shown that these linguistic behaviours are indeed what senior men and women are doing in certain large corporations, as I discuss later in this chapter. However, as long as stereotypical masculinity and femininity continue to be prized by hegemonic discourses that privilege gender *difference,* such a freedom will remain hard to achieve, and may not even be valued in the organisation.

In challenging the monolithic character of beliefs grounded in naive assumptions around the 'essential truth' of gender difference, the discourse approach has even contested the category of 'woman'. This category is viewed as highly unstable, in the sense that it is difficult to generalise about what being a woman is (Butler 1990; Cameron 1997). Moreover, the early feminist notion that there is a universal womanly nature has itself been firmly questioned (see Baxter 2003 for overview). Just as there are many inconsistencies and contradictions *within* any individual woman, there are always differences *between* women, often governed by their age, social group, family background, education, and so on. Overall, the social constructionist approach suggests that gendered identities and roles are not open to generalisation or easy categorisation. They are not fixed and static but shifting, fragmentary, multiple, frequently contradictory and constantly in the process of being constituted and negotiated through linguistic interactions.

So how does discourse theory link up the role of institutional discourses with the social construction of gendered identities? According to the Foucauldian theorist, Brewis (2001), identities are constructed through discourses; people are never outside 'discourses', but always answerable to them and constituted by them. Like Butler (1990), her position on this is quite radical:

> If we accept that gender is a discursive category – i.e. that there is no biological basis to masculinity or femininity as sets of behaviours, attitudes and experiences – then we must accept that there is nothing authentically 'feminine' about women, that they are constituted as such by discourse.
>
> (Brewis 2001: 293)

This implies that discourses are responsible for producing a range of reaffirmable subject positions that form the basis of people's personal, social and professional identities. So if gendered discourses generally position women as less suited to organisational life because they are stereotyped as more irrational, emotional and subjective in their decision-making than men, over time this will have an effect on the way in which women will inevitably speak and act.

However, two features of social constructionist theory mediate this rather deterministic perspective, and allow for some sense of 'self', presence or personhood. As discussed above, first, people have the agency to resist and overturn such compliant subject positioning, and secondly, people are never uniformly positioned by single discourses but always shifting between multiple and competing subject positions or selves. In my own research (Baxter 2003), I have shown that leaders are constantly moving between different positions of power within organisations. They may be very powerful in one subject position as (say) a head of department, but may be much less powerful in another position, for example, in their role as a board director because they may lack experience, or are in charge of a less prestigious function.

So in sum, why is the discourse approach useful for discussing leaders' language in the Gender-Multiple corporation? First, it suggests that male and female leaders are not bound to use language in pre-fixed ways according to their gender, but have the flexibility to use a *repertoire* of speech strategies and behaviours traditionally coded 'masculine' and 'feminine'. Second, discourse theory is useful because it warns us that hegemonic discourses of gender difference can have enormous power within the organisation, and can be responsible for invoking negative and discriminatory expectations of women and female leaders in particular. However, thirdly, discourse theory explains that female leaders have the agency to resist and overturn potentially 'damaging' (Sunderland 2004) discourses that discriminate on the grounds of gender. Indeed, without this kind of resistance, no change would ever be effected, and patently, organisations do change. Fourth, discourse theory considers that no individual is uniformly powerless at any level in the organisation (although forms of systematic powerlessness do occur; see Baxter 2003). Clearly, senior women do have more power than subordinate female employees in terms of formal status, but there may be other ways in which their power is systematically undermined – by sexist attitudes, by social snobbery, professional rivalry, and so on. Female leaders have the agency, indeed the opportunity to manoeuvre between different subject positions within their organisations, some of which may generate considerable power, and others of which may need contesting in order for them to become more effective.

Discourse theory is particularly appropriate for explaining how female leaders operate in the Gender-Multiple corporation because its principles support the notion of fluid gender roles, diverse talent, constant organisational change, ways of achieving self-empowerment, and the value of linguistic expertise at leadership level. We now see how contexts or specifically, communities of practice also shape the interactions of leaders.

Communities of practice (CofPs)

Language and gender researchers such as Marra, Schnurr and Holmes (2006) have successfully used the concept of CofPs to analyse female leadership contexts. The CofP approach is compatible with the social constructionist view of gender because of its interest in *actions* and *process* as the means of constructing communities. Cameron (1996: 45) explains why the two approaches are theoretically compatible:

> Throughout our lives we go on entering new communities of practice: we must constantly produce our gendered identities by

performing what are taken to be the appropriate acts in the communities we belong to – or else challenge prevailing gender norms by refusing to perform those acts.

The original concept of the 'community of practice' (Lave and Wenger 1991) was promoted within language and gender research by Eckert and McConnell-Ginet (1998: 464) who defined it as:

> An aggregate of people who come together around mutual engagement in an endeavour. Ways of doing things, ways of talking, beliefs, values, power relations – in short, practices – emerge in the course of this mutual endeavour. As a social construct, a CofP is different from the traditional community, primarily because it is defined simultaneously by its membership and by the practice in which that membership engages.

It was further defined by Wenger (1998: 76) as constituted by three crucial dimensions:

- Mutual engagement
- A jointly negotiated enterprise
- A shared repertoire of negotiable resources accumulated over time

A community of practice might take the concrete form of a departmental team meeting, a main board meeting, an interview context, a disciplinary hearing, a regular social activity for employees, and so on. So, if we take a meeting of company directors as an example, this community of practice could be defined in terms of:

- its regular participants (the main board directors),
- the setting (the regular room where these members meet),
- the topic of the meeting (e.g. strategic planning)
- the purpose: (making decisions about strategy and how this will be achieved)

The value of the CofP approach to analysing leadership interactions is the 'focus it affords on the mutually constitutive nature of the individual, group, activity and meaning' (Eckert 2000: 35). In terms of female leadership, it offers a means of understanding how the relationship between leadership and gender is routinely negotiated through social practices within a range of familiar contexts. Individual members can be 'core' or 'peripheral' depending on their status, and how well integrated they are within the community. Eckert and McConnell-Ginet (1998: 95) consider that individuals and CofPs change constantly with each interaction, and that people's gendered identities are transformed as they negotiate different 'forms of femininity, masculinity and gender relations'. This viewpoint fits well with the construct of a Gender-Multiple corporation, where the identities (or 'selves') of leaders would be constantly in flux, as leaders use a diverse range of interactional strategies to assert their authority and accomplish complex and ever-changing goals. CofPs also reflect and help to constitute a particular corporate culture through these on-going practices. Marra, Schnurr and Holmes (2006) suggest that in traditional, hierarchical organisations, leaders may tend to use more masculine or transactional strategies in their CofPs, whereas in egalitarian organisations, leaders will go for more feminine or relational strategies. Provisional research pertaining to the construct of the Gender-Multiple corporation, has shown that these are more likely to be egalitarian in structure and culture, and their CofPs would be characterised by diverse, pragmatic and ever-changing strategies as they respond to the different needs of the business (Baxter 2008; Mullany 2007; Schnurr 2008).

Drawing on these three sets of insights of the discourse approach – discourses in the corporation, social construction of gender, and the concept of CofPs, I will now turn to some of the research that demonstrates how both senior men and women are transforming the way they use leadership language in the Gender-Multiple corporation, and thus making it a rich and rewarding place for female leaders to work.

Leadership language

The feminisation of the male leader?

Over the last couple of decades, an increasing number of *male* leaders have advocated their interest in a more 'relational' approach to leadership (that is, a concern to express how one feels, and to build and maintain good relationships with others (Fletcher 1999; Holmes 2006). There are strong hints of this in a classic article by William H. Peace, a US businessman, who gave his vote to an alternative style of leadership to the classic 'command and control':

> I am a soft manager. Unlike the classic leaders of business legend with their towering self-confidence, their unflinching tenacity, their hard, lonely lives at the top, I try to be vulnerable to crit-icism, I do my best to be tentative, and I cherish my share of human frailty...in my vocabulary, soft management does not mean weak management.
>
> (Peace 2001: 99)

At no point in his discussion does Peace explicitly conceptualise his leadership style as 'femininised', and arguably, it is purely co-incidental that the 'feminine' leadership style can be aligned with the relational style at all (Holmes 2006). Yet Cameron (1995), among others, has made the case that the male business estab-lishment, having seen the pragmatic value of the 'feminine' rela-tional style to effective leadership, must aim to appropriate it. To be successful, such appropriation must contest any negative con-notations of the feminine leadership style and reassign it with new, more positive, gender-neutral meanings. This is indeed implied in Peace's proposition above that 'soft management does not mean weak management' (2001: 99). In similar spirit, John Kotter (2001: 85) argues that there are two 'distinctive and complementary systems of action': *leadership* and *management*, both necessary for success in 'an increasingly complex and volatile business envi-ronment'. However, he argues that the leader-manager role is too much for one person; these are different functions. For Kotter, *leadership*, the superior expertise, is associated with transformational skills: coping with change and complexity in a more compet-itive and volatile world, offering a vision, setting a direction and motivating and inspiring subordinates. *Management*, in contrast, is viewed as the inferior expertise and largely transactional: achiev-ing order and consistency to key functions such as the quality and profitability of products, planning and budgeting, organ-ising and staffing, and controlling and problem-solving. In this spirit, Kotter elevates the transformational elements of leadership to an almost mystical level, despite insisting that 'there is no magic in it':

> Leadership is different. Achieving grand visions always requires a burst of energy. Motivation and inspiration energise people, not by pushing them in the right direction as control mechanisms do but by satisfying basic human instincts for achievement, a sense of belonging, recognition, self-esteem, a feeling of control over one's life, and the ability to live up to one's ideals. Such feelings touch us deeply and elicit a powerful response.
>
> (Kotter 2001: 93)

Kotter's comment above implies that 'relational' elements, such as the leadership imperative to engage with the feelings of colleagues and subordinates, are a crucial part of this broader 'transformational' leadership style. Again, there is no explicit gendering in the language used by Kotter to describe the ideal business leader, but arguably, there is an appropriation of terms traditionally associated with a more feminine leadership style. It could be argued that the language associated with the relational style is gender-neutral, associated merely with the classic binary division of reason over emotion. Bales' (1951) early work on the nature of leadership did indeed identify two dimensions of leadership (the task-orientated expert and socio-emotional expert), which were not connected in any way to gender – until a little later (e.g. Lockheed and Hall 1976; Strodtbeck and Mann 1956). But as I argued above, this conceptual division (transactional/relational) has also been historically attached to the perceived biological and socio-cultural divisions between males and females, and such deeply-entrenched connotations are likely to operate on a sub-conscious level for most people when they are making sense of leadership styles and language. In order for a relational leadership style to be deemed acceptable to the majority of male senior leaders brought up with the archetype of heroic leadership (Olsson 2006), it must be to an extent de-feminised.

My own research (Baxter 2008) reflects that, in their public rhetoric at least, male senior managers have 're-engineered' the more expressive, feminine, relational dimension to make it seem generic to leadership. I asked ten male and ten female senior managers from large, multi-national companies, to identify the types of speech they considered most appropriate for working with their seniors, with their peers and with subordinates (see Appendix 2). I now explore the responses of the *male* managers to show how far from the traditional 'command and control' model of leadership these leaders have moved.

The data seem to indicate that an appropriation of a relational style of leadership is taking place, or at least an acknowledgement that modern day leaders need a much more diverse range of communicative strategies than in the past. For example, almost all the respondents advocated the need to express personal respect, mutual trust, regard for the contribution that other team members can bring, and the development of individual and diverse talents. A common theme in the data, for example, was the ability to be *a good listener*:

> (1) 'It's every sense of listening; it's not just listening to the words people say, but what they are meaning and trying to sense the energy with which they are saying them. Far too often, the more senior you are, you stop listening and that's absolutely lethal. Because until you're hearing, you don't know what arguments are being made, where they're coming from...'
>
> (Male CEO; mobile phone company)

Another common theme in the data (Baxter 2008) was the need to be *'open'* with others – a frequently occurring 'buzzword', and a value that is also explicitly stated in the company mission statements I examined. Among other things, 'being open' seemed to mean 'being prepared to admit mistakes' to lower ranking employees:

> (2) 'Actually, what really brings people on your side is if you make mistakes and say 'I got that wrong once' and if you're expressing your feelings, being *open*, they suddenly see why they might connect with this person rather than that. They think, 'I've made a mistake like that and it's OK to say so, and it makes them want to engage with you more.'
>
> (Male CEO; telecommunications company)

The speaker's own use of language (use of the connecting pronoun 'you'; the use of reported speech) invites the listener to participate vicariously in the experiences which he describes. Such strategies encourage us to empathise and engage with the speaker, and indicate that he is being sincere in what he says. When male leaders were asked which styles of communication they would *least* tend to use with colleagues at different levels, a number of the respondents mentioned 'establishing status':

(3) 'You don't need to establish your position. Nobody wants to hear the ten-minute verbal CV. You're there because you're there. They know you're the boss. Promoting yourself smacks to me of insecurity. You do get it among newly promoted people when it's quite unnecessary.'
(Male Marketing SVP, computer software company)

There was a similar attitude towards the stereotypical masculine trait of 'being confrontational', which was roundly condemned by most of my male respondents as counter-productive:

(4) 'My approach is to avoid personal confrontation at all costs, not to have too many enemies, and so conversely, I think being polite and courteous is very important. You meet the same people on the way up as you do on the way down, so there is no point falling out with people permanently.'
(Sales SVP; information design company)

In their rhetoric at least, these managers were keen to distance themselves from 'transactional' or stereotypically masculine leadership traits. In the following, this male executive graphically caricatures the old-style manager in order to distance himself from such a portrait:

(5) 'If you are to adopt the demeanour of a typical sales director, table-thumping, hard-swearing, hard-drinking, fast motorway driving, you won't make it to the boardroom because you have to represent the company. Investors want to feel that if you are going to fail, fail elegantly. It's an old adage but it works.'
(Marketing Director; electronics company)

So, my findings initially suggested that, in bucking the stereotypes, *male* directors were concerned to position themselves within a *relational* discourse of leadership. Yet, I found that this wasn't the whole story. As Example (3) above indicates, the surface public rhetoric is at times undercut by competing messages in terms of delivery style, imagery, or sub-textual nuances. In other words, these male managers were often quite unaware that they offered more traditionally *masculine* speaker identities in their narratives. One Marketing SVP, having stated there was no place for self-promotion, uses a series of short, parallel statements in which the key phrase 'I speak' is repeated three times, to emphasise his subject position as an important and influential senior manager:

> (6) 'I speak to Australia all the time. I spoke to Italy this morning. I speak daily to different countries round the world. My reach is truly global.'
>
> (Marketing SVP, telecommunications company)

There was also a lot of name-dropping and references to elite personalities from certain respondents. In this utterance, the initial shift from second to first person pronoun (from 'you' to 'I') implies that the generic 'superman manager' is in fact the speaker:

> (7) 'You have to be able to deal with any level of person with equal facility. I've recently dined with the Chancellor of the Exchequer, the Hungarian Prime Minister, the Italian Prime Minister and the Czech Foreign Minister. If you can't make those adjustments, you won't cut the mustard.'
>
> (CEO; mobile phone company)

The imagery within participants' narratives was often explicitly gendered. This was noticeable in the common use of masculinised sporting metaphors (see Chapter 2):

> (8) 'An effective leader is always born, never made. It's the old thing; you can't train a striker. You can either score goals or you can't.'
>
> (Marketing director, electronics company)

My conclusion to this analysis is to suggest that while male leaders are highly alert to the need to demonstrate a range of values and identities, clearly privileging relational leadership in what they say, a closer study of their use of language shows that a 'masculine' speech style continues to undercut and supplement the consciously per-formed identity of a 'caring' and 'open' manager. Perhaps the current fashion for male leaders stating that they align themselves with a rela-tional leadership style isn't wholly borne out in linguistic analysis? Or perhaps this favouring of the relational is just a fashion rather than a deeper change in male leadership style? Alternatively, it might be a genuine index of how the male manager aspires to lead within the Gender-Multiple corporation: an encouraging sign for the future. Indeed, the 'feminisation' of the male leader may be a vital first step in enabling the Gender-Multiple corporation to be *talked* into being. This can only be of mutual benefit to female leaders in the longer term.

Evidence that the Gender-Multiple corporation is becoming a reality is heralded by further research on the ways in which both senior men and women use a diverse range of linguistic strategies in order to accomplish leadership successfully.

Female leadership and linguistic repertoire

Recent language and gender studies on the workplace (e.g. Holmes and Stubbe 2003; Holmes 2006; Mullany 2007; Schnurr 2008) have argued that effective leaders draw from a wide *repertoire* of com-municative strategies to achieve their goals. Taking the social con-structionist perspective that leadership is an *activity* rather than just attributes or outcomes, these studies suggest that both male and female leaders deploy enormous skill in selecting the appropriate interactional style for a particular context – running a formal meet-ing, mixing with employees in the bar, handling a disciplinary matter, hosting an informal dinner with an overseas client, and so on.

The leading exponent of the 'repertoire' approach is Janet Holmes (2006) and her team in New Zealand who run the Language in the Workplace Project (LWP), serving the dual interests of academic research and developing good business practice. This approach posits that effective leaders have developed a wide linguistic repertoire from which they select appropriate strategies according to con-textual factors. Leaders are skilled in integrating transactional with relational factors and will vary their choice of style depending on context and community of practice (CofPs). Rather than describing leadership styles as gendered, Holmes and her colleagues (Marra,

Schnurr and Holmes 2006) have argued that the contexts or CofPs within which they work are gendered:

> New Zealanders readily describe workplaces as more or less 'feminine' and more or less 'masculine' in orientation. Rather than simply referring to the gender composition of the group, however, the gendered labels refer to the practices, including communicative practices consistent with the Communities of Practice framework.
>
> (Marra, Schnurr and Holmes 2006: 243)

The authors argue that a workplace team which displays predominantly feminine interactional patterns such as a collaborative style, an egalitarian philosophy, and who are routinely indirect and supportive of one another might represent the more feminine end of the workplace spectrum, whereas a team who are competitive, individualistic and challenging would be considered to represent the more masculine end of the spectrum. This is irrespective of the biological sex composition of team members.

The work of Holmes and her colleagues has also shown how individual female managers skilfully deploy interactional styles that range along this continuum depending on contextual factors such as the participants, topic, purpose and setting. Selecting two female leaders as their examples, (Clara and Tricia, both pseudonyms), Marra, Schnurr and Holmes (2006) show how Clara's leadership style is consistent with the relatively masculine orientation of the CofP in which she operates. Clara leads a team of approximately 50 people in the New Zealand division of a large multi-national corporation. According to Marra, Schnurr and Holmes (2006: 245), Clara's team has a 'sparky, interactional style which is "individualistic" and "competitive", a description consistent with the masculine stereotypes described in the literature'. Clara herself plays up to the role of 'Queen' (see Chapter 2 on role models for female leaders, but here the term is used playfully and ironically), and indeed she is analysed as behaving in a relatively authoritarian way in the context of a regular weekly meeting with her project team:

(*Key:* Har=Harold; Cla=Clara; Pe=Peggy)

1   **Har:** look's like there's been actually a request for screendumps
2   I know it was outside of the scope
3   but people will be pretty worried about it

4   **Cla:** no screendumps
5   **Matt:** we-
6   **Cla:** no screendumps
7   **Peg:** [sarcastically] thank you Clara
8   **Cla:** /no screendumps\
9   **Matt:** /we know\ we know you didn't want them and we um er /we've\
10   **Cla:** /that does not\ meet the criteria

(Holmes 2006: 57)

Here Clara is 'doing power' explicitly and baldly, using aggravated directives ('no screendumps'), and apparently disregarding conventional politeness. This implies that her authority is historically accepted by the group, and that she is expected to use it. However, in the context of a different CofP, the regular weekly meeting of another team into which she has been drafted as the usual chairperson is absent, her manner is very different:

(*Key*: Ren=Renee)

1   **Cla:** okay well we might just start without Seth
2   he can come in and can review the minutes from last week
3   **Ren:** are you taking the minutes this week
4   **Cla:** no I'm just trying to chair the meeting
5   who would like to take minutes this week
6   **Ren:** who hasn't taken the minutes yet
7   **Ben:** I haven't yet I will
8   **Cla:** thank you /Benny\
9   **Ren:** /oh Benny\ takes beautiful minutes too
10   **Ben:** don't tell them they'll want me doing it every week
11   [*general laughter*]
12   **Cla:** it's a bit of a secret
13   okay shall we kick off and just go round the room um doing an update
14   and then when Seth comes in with the minutes
15   we need to check on any action items from our planning
16   over to you Marlene

(Holmes 2006: 245–246)

Here, Clara's manner is seen to be much more informal and relaxed, indicated by her use of gentle humour ('it's a bit of a secret') and her consistent use of politeness, even though there is no question of who is in charge. Clara's interactional style within the context of a 'masculinised' CofP is contrasted with the style of Tricia, below, who is the supervisor of about 100 staff in a non-profit organisation in Wellington. Tricia is shown to have a much more unobtrusive management style in a more overtly democratic organisation, which is reflected in her fortnightly management meeting. She successfully opens her meeting using a non-threatening and non-authoritarian style, which minimises displays of power and emphasises colleagiality. Marra, Schnurr and Holmes (2006) argue that this particular approach allows her to balance transactional and relational goals as appropriate to her CofP.

The studies of Holmes and her colleagues demonstrate how, through a repertoire approach to leadership interactional styles, a Gender-Multiple corporation can be almost literally *talked* into being. This school of theory can sometimes make a too easy equation between 'doing femininity' and achieving relational goals, which actually suggests that the linguistic repertoire isn't as open or as gender-multiple as it might appear in their theorisation (see Schnurr 2008). In other words, their argument implies that female leaders use the relational aspects of leadership to assert their identity as biological females and being culturally recognised as women. Despite this slight implication of essentialism in their argument, the Holmes approach does remind us that discourses of gender difference cannot be lightly dismissed, and will continue to influence the behaviour of female leaders, even in the Gender-Multiple corporation, as long as these discourses remain culturally dominant in western society. This point is endorsed by Mullany (2007) whose work reaches very similar conclusions to those of Holmes and her team: that male and female use 'masculine' and 'feminine' discursive strategies equally effectively to achieve their objectives. However, Mullany (*ibid*) adds a further dimension with her discussion of gendered discourses. She argues that potentially 'damaging' gendered discourses (Sunderland 2004) filtering through the organisations she studied (such as *female emotionality/irrationality, image and sexuality* and *career progression and motherhood*, worked against senior women in highly negative ways. She found that these discourses were used as a lens to judge female leaders more harshly than their male counterparts, regardless of their apparently effective use of a repertoire of linguistic skills.

To explore these points further and to demonstrate how female executives can gain or lose power, I now turn to a study using the discourse approach to leadership language (Baxter 2003). Analysing female leadership language in relation to diverse, *competing* discourses helps us to understand how the Gender-Multiple corporation can offer female leaders a better chance to be effective than if they worked in other types of corporation where gendered discourses prevail unchallenged.

Competing discourses

I conducted an ethnographic study (Baxter 2003) of a well-known internet company in the UK, whose job was to sell products such as cars, homes and jobs on the internet. The main board comprised a team of seven managers, one of whom was the only woman (Sarah). The company was proud of its diversity policies, operated a flattened organisational structure with devolved responsibilities, and had equal numbers of males and females at middle management level. It had a mission statement of encouraging openness in the organisation: encouraging frank exchanges and being prepared to listen to and support all the employees in their respective functions.

In the spirit of ethnographic study, I spent some time observing interactions in a series of routine management meetings. Across my corpus of data, I identified four dominant institutional discourses that seemed to position speakers in different and asymmetrical ways. These were:

- *Historical legacy* (how long each director had been at the company);
- *Competing specialisms* (the comparative importance of each business function in relation to the other functions);
- *Open dialogue* (an encouragement of a frank and open exchange of ideas and views);
- *Masculinisation* (a gendered discourse promoting dominance, rivalry, toughness, aggression and goal-orientated action).

These competing discourses entailed certain constraints on individual speech and behaviour but also granted opportunities for people to gain influence and empowerment. In many ways the company fitted the description of a Gender-Multiple corporation except in one key respect: because the board was almost entirely masculine, this had perhaps inadvertently opened the way for a discourse of masculinisation, which made Sarah's job as the only woman much more challenging.

In the following extract, the team is discussing the fact that there has been an operations failure the previous day, causing a whole range of problems, not least between members of the senior team:

1	SARAH:	I didn't understand you were having those experiences (.) and I sit next to you
2		(*laughs*) I knew what we were doing (.) I knew we were having issues (.) but I did not
3		understand that user issues were absolutely appalling (.) nobody told me
4		(7)
5	JACK:	well I just thought the site was down all day you [see
6	SARAH:	[we did communicate to everybody when it was back up
7	KEITH:	could we have some way of making sure when the site is back up (1)
8	SARAH:	yeah well the guys upstairs would have been aware but I'm just saying that I wasn't (1) it
9		isn't as if they would get it back up and ignore it you know get it back up and just walk
10		away it doesn't work that way
11	JACK:	that's why I just assumed that if the guys upstairs (.) if they were having problems with it(.)
12		[they...
13	SARAH:	[the guys upstairs understand it but you're asking (*continuing to talk over*
14		*the others*) you're asking for a different interpretation to different people (.) which is fine
15		(.) but I just need to be aware of that and this discussion is absolutely fine (*silence*
16		*among whole meeting for several seconds*)

In this extract, Sarah is positioned as a relatively powerful member of the team in relation to her colleagues. In terms of contextual information, Sarah was one of the two founder members of the company and currently the IT Director, which was a highly regarded role, giving her a structurally powerful position in terms of the discourse of *historical legacy* and *competing specialisms*. She was also powerfully positioned in terms of the two other discourses as I now show.

At the start of this extract, Sarah is being held to account by Jack, the Marketing Director, for the operations failure. Sarah is verbally dominant, saying more than any of her colleagues. She also uses adversarial and confrontational language indicated by bald assertions ('nobody told me'), frank judgements ('it was absolutely appalling') implicit directives ('I just need to be aware...'), and interruptions (see ll. 6 and 12). The use of language typifies a discourse of *masculinisation* in this community of practice, where males and females are expected equally to use a stereotypically masculine style of speech, and Sarah appears to do this here. She is also powerfully positioned in terms of the discourse of *open dialogue*: she is very direct in telling Keith (the Managing Director) that he was at fault in not communicating the scale of the problem (l.1: 'I didn't understand you were having those experiences and I sit next to you'). However, masculinisation can potentially compete with a discourse of open dialogue: while masculinisation tends to encourage assertiveness and competitiveness between team members, open dialogue in contrast is supposed to foster co-operativeness and understanding between employees. Here Sarah is arguably masculinising her use of open dialogue, and thus neutralising it, to defend her position and to criticise her colleagues.

So while Sarah appears to be relatively powerfully positioned as the only female member of the team in terms of all four discourses during this extract, it is also clear that she isn't uniformly powerful, and we might wish to ask why this is. Note that towards the end of the extract, extended silences tend to greet Sarah's utterances. This is in keeping with language and gender research (e.g. DeFrancisco 1991) which argues that men tend to greet assertive or masculinised talk by women with *silence* as a form of protest. There were tensions between Sarah and other members of the team, which are indicated here in Jack's insistent cross-questioning of her. In sum, while Sarah appears to be a powerful and assimilated member of this team, and indeed, was demonstrably so according to this brief discourse analysis, there are also indications that her position of power is resented and to a certain extent, resisted by her male colleagues.

Using a discourse approach helps to make sense of the way female leaders like Sarah achieve a considerable degree of powerfulness despite, and perhaps because of, the gendered discourses (such as *masculinisation*) circulating within any organisation. As we saw in Chapter 2, female leaders are judged more harshly than men for using a masculinised discourse. It is clear that, even in a Gender-Multiple corporation such as this, the relationship between female leaders and their positioning by gendered discourses can offer women a strong position, but still be problematic. However, there are clear opportunities for contesting such discourses where competing discourses circulate, and Sarah was strongly positioned to do exactly that.

Sarah was demonstrating specific linguistic expertise to be effective in her organisation. This is a theme I now pursue in a case study of senior executives in the next chapter.

5
Case Study 1: Linguistic Work in the Corporation

Introduction

This chapter and the next explore some of the linguistic strategies female leaders have evolved to succeed in different types of corporation. I argue that senior women have developed a special kind of linguistic expertise or 'work' that they must do in order to be viewed by their peers and subordinates as effective leaders. It is likely that their male colleagues are entirely unaware of the extra linguistic work women do, as generally, they do not have to make this effort themselves. My research experience shows that women leaders demonstrate a much greater concern with the *impact* of their language on others than male leaders do (Baxter 2008). This is because male leaders do not *need* to have the same concern with the impact of their gender, particularly in male-dominated contexts. In many ways senior women have learnt to *hone* the ways in which they interact with colleagues on different levels and grades. However, this use of a special kind of linguistic expertise did not seem to affect relationships with clients to the same extent, where differences in role and relationship were more clearly contrasted and defined (*ibid*). In both Male-Dominated and Gender-Divided corporations, I argue that the need for linguistic expertise for senior women is essential for their survival but may well prove self-defeating in some contexts as we shall see. In the case study that follows, I consider the range of linguistic strategies that senior women from a number of top UK multinational companies say they use, and the perceived *impact* of this on their roles and performance as leaders. Based on this research evidence, I suggest that developing such linguistic expertise could support women performing senior management roles, especially in the Gender-Multiple corporation.

Theoretical approach

The following case study is part of an on-going research project investigating whether linguistic interactions might be considered a significant reason for the under-representation of female leaders at board level in the UK (e.g. Baxter 2008). The primary purpose of the case study was to explore the ways in which senior people construct their sense of leadership identities (how they see themselves as leaders; how they think they are perceived by others; how they actually perform leadership) through their language use. The case study was conducted in order to address the overall project aim: to find out whether the use of leadership language can help to explain the under-representation of women leaders in the business world.

The study was broadly conducted from a discourse perspective (see Chapter 4), which considers that the construction of leadership identities ('doing' leadership) interacts with institutional discourses, including discourses on gender, which help to define roles, relationships, procedures, practices, attitudes, norms and values within any organisation. Critical to this 'dialogic' process (Bakhtin 1929/ 1981) is the role of language in enabling such interactions to take place and in constructing social and professional processes and outcomes. To put it much more simply, individuals constantly 'work out' their professional identities in the workplace through language, and this matters because their success or failure can be dependent on it.

A key theoretical principle which governed the analysis of the findings of the case study is that of *double-voiced discourse*, taken originally from Mikhail Bakhtin (1929/1981) but adapted by the language and gender theorist, Amy Sheldon (1992). This is the idea that when we speak we are not simply expressing our own needs and goals (*single-voiced discourse*), but we are also taking into account the needs and goals of our addressees and constantly modifying what we say in the light of it. So those who use 'double-voiced discourse' are continuously fine-tuning their own use of language, and judging the impact of it, in relation to what others have to say. Sheldon describes double-voiced discourse as:

> The perspective-taking stance of [the] style in which the speaker expresses a double orientation or double alignment. The primary orientation is to the self, to one's own agenda. The other orientation is to the members of the group. The orientation to others does not mean that the speaker necessarily acts in an altruistic, accommodating or even self-sacrificing manner. It means rather that the speaker pays attention to the companion's point of view, even while pursuing her own agenda. As a result the voice of the self is enmeshed with and regulated by the voice of the other.
>
> (Sheldon 1992: 9)

Sheldon's theory of 'double-voiced discourse' was originally applied to the analysis of American, middle class, white girls' 'conflict talk', which she characterised as having a dual orientation in that speakers negotiated their own agenda while simultaneously orienting towards the viewpoint of their partner. This she contrasted with 'single-voiced discourse', where the voice is 'free-standing, not enmeshed with, or regulated by the voice of the other, and therefore is easier to hear' (Sheldon 1992: 100). This use of single-voiced discourse, Sheldon identified as especially characteristic of *male* conflict-talk, which exhibited a single-minded commitment to pursuing one's own agenda. The interesting feature about double-voiced discourse is that it is *not* some simple re-categorisation of 'feminine', co-operative talk (e.g. Coates 2004; Tannen 1994a), which has the primary goal of engaging with 'the other'. Rather, if we consider the business context, its primary goal is to achieve one's objectives by *co-opting* co-operative strategies for a strategic purpose. While single-voiced discourse is a relatively overt or explicit means of pursuing one's own agenda, double-voiced discourse might be perceived as a more covert and potentially a more manipulative means of interaction. Sheldon (1992) argues that her analysis of double-voiced discourse *could* tend to support the gendered stereotype of females as more duplicitous, cunning and underhand than males. But she also suggests an alternative reading: that females need to find ways of achieving their own aims that avoid direct confrontation with others (Maltz and Borker 1982).

According to Sheldon (*ibid*), this female quest to avoid direct conflict requires a high degree of preparation, subtlety, reflection, sensitivity and additional *energy* in order for interactions with others to be effective.

This theory of double-voiced discourse shows how the enmeshing of the voice of the self with the voice of the other can lead to social benefits of greater affiliation and solidarity between the speaker and addressee. However, Sheldon (1992: 101) argues that as a result, the female voice 'can be harder to hear'. By this she means that the primary message – achieving a particular goal such as getting someone to do something – might be less loud and clear than by the means of single-voiced discourse because the intention of the speaker may be misread or misinterpreted, and the impact of the message may be lost. But this is necessarily the *effect* of double-voiced discourse: the speaker may have very similar intentions to the person using single-voiced discourse; they just hope to accomplish their objective by less obvious and more nuanced means.

Methodology

The case study was conducted in two stages. The *first* stage, aimed at eliciting senior people's perceptions of their leadership identities, involved conducting audio-recorded interviews with 20 business leaders from UK multi-national companies, ten of whom were female and ten of whom were male. The *second* stage, learning about the linguistic construction of leadership through actual performance, was to observe and record a series of business meetings (see Chapter 6). The case study in this chapter examines the *first* stage: the interview narratives of these leaders.

Pichler (2008) has argued that there are limitations in drawing inferences about identity construction from respondents' perceptions gleaned purely from interview narratives rather than interactive events, as these should not be regarded as 'transparent' data. However, interviews are arguably as valid a social/research context as any other, particularly when considering the identities that subjects tend to explicitly 'claim or disclaim' for themselves within the interview format (Cameron and Kulick 2003). In order that these accounts are not read simply as transparent 'windows' on respondents' identities, I subjected the narratives to various forms of linguistic analysis consistent with the discourse approach (Derrida 1987), as detailed below.

The interviews were conducted on-site, over a period of up to two hours with each senior person. I aimed to make the interview questions as generalised and open-ended as possible, using only brief prompts to encourage narrative flow and continuity. I deliberately avoided asking specific questions about gender, or indeed, implying that there might be gender differences between male and female leaders. This is partly because I wanted to avoid a leading or 'loaded' questioning approach, and more importantly, it would only serve to endorse the notion of gender as a super-ordinate factor in constructing people's identities, which the discourse approach has sought to challenge (Butler 1990). Where subjects did make unprompted claims on behalf of gender, I deduced that this might indeed signify that particular discourses (such as gender difference) were shaping the perceptions and experiences of the speaker (Swann 2002).

In order to meet the primary aim of the research (see above), the case study had two quite pragmatic objectives:

(1) To collect and assess the viewpoints of male and female senior managers on the importance of different types of spoken interaction for accomplishing business leadership effectively;

(2) To explore the ways in which senior people linguistically construct their sense of leadership identities through their narratives about leadership experiences.

In order to achieve the first objective, I set each subject two tasks as prompts for more open discussion, neither of which fore-grounded gender in any obvious way. The first task was a sheet (see Appendix 2) listing 'Linguistic features of leadership' which had been derived inductively from a previous study (Baxter 2003). I asked each participant to select and comment on the three features they saw to be the *most* important to conducting effective leadership, and the three features they saw to be the *least* important, when working with four groups of people:

- People on the grade above (where relevant)
- People of an equal grade

- People in their 'team'
- Clients/suppliers

The second task was to ask the participants to comment on 'The Language of Corporate Culture' (see Appendix 3), which was characterised in two columns as Transactional (labelled only as 'A' for participants) or Relational (labelled only as 'B' for participants). These categories were derived from a range of literature by organisation behaviourists in female leadership (e.g. Bass and Avolio 1993; Vinnicombe and Singh 2002). The lists of key words associated with each column (e.g. *growth, profit, delivery* in the 'A' column) were derived both from: the cited literature, documentation from participants' companies giving mission statements, and also ethnographically, from my previous study (Baxter 2003). As I have argued so far, the overarching terms of 'transactional' and 'relational' are deemed to be meaningful categories as ways of conceptualising values and behaviours within corporate culture and therefore as an appropriate springboard for interviewee responses.

With the audio-recorded interview data, the approach to analysis was to identify patterns of language use which appeared to signify interviewee support for transactional discourses, relational discourses, evidence of both, or indeed, alternative discourses, which would help to understand the allegiance of senior people to different styles of leadership. This identification often centred around the use of the key words listed to describe the two discourses, or relied upon more formal methods of textual and linguistic analysis. This analysis involved a description of lexico-grammatical and discoursal features (e.g. Baxter 2003; Sunderland 2004), including the prevalent use of metaphor (Koller 2004), which were then used as a basis to deduce linguistic markers of identity, personal agendas, implied power relationships between people, as well as similarities and differences between male and female leaders in their perceptions of how to 'do' leadership effectively.

Findings of the study

Overall, it was interesting to discover that there are many commonalities between the ways in which male and female leaders say they use language to 'do leadership' effectively. This supports the research I described in Chapter 4, which argues that the nature of today's leadership requires male and female leaders to be equally capable of drawing on a 'repertoire' of speech and interactional strategies, 'transactional', 'relational' and combined, in order to be 'up to speed' in a fast-paced, pragmatic and globalised business environment. Male leaders therefore say they use strategies traditionally coded 'feminine' such as listening, admitting weaknesses, being open about their feelings and views, and soliciting the opinions of subordinates. Female leaders say they deploy strategies coded masculine in order to be assertive, confrontational and goal-driven, as required by business context or purpose.

An important feature of the data is that transactional and relational styles of leadership are closely intertwined. Males and females equally use 'relational practices' (Fletcher 1999) in order to achieve transactional goals, although the apparent opposite (using transactional strategies to achieve relational or transformational goals) does not seem to be a feature for either sex. Both males and females single out the value of 'plain speaking' and the need to be open about a range of professional matters.

However there was something distinctive about the *female* data that I hadn't expected. The women expressed a strong awareness of the *way* they used language that seemed to be associated explicitly with their gender. This was denoted by participants' use of self-referentiality: specifically, in this case, referring to the way they used language to deal with their minority status among men. From the overall analysis of the data, I found that women leaders repeatedly expressed concern about the impact of their language use – *as women* – upon their professional colleagues. While this is perhaps at odds with their sense of pragmatic, context-driven, professional role, these senior women stated that they *had* to do something different in their talk from men. They expressed how they carried out linguistic work in terms of observing, regulating, policing, reviewing and repairing their spoken contributions within institutional settings. They seem to be consciously assessing how they appear in the eyes of the masculine 'other', and constantly aiming to prepare, pre-judge or *pre-empt* negative evaluations of their work. In this female executive's comment, she makes explicit reference to gender in suggesting that she has to carry out a lot of work, literally and metaphorically, to prepare for a meeting where she is the only woman present:

> (1) 'If it is an all-male meeting, I make sure that I have done my homework and I have prepared what my main points are, so I do a fairly careful analysis of what I think other people's agendas are going to be and how that impacts on what my own agenda is, and how I'm going to deal with their objectives.'
>
> (Financial SVP, engineering company)

One of the key themes in the data was senior women's perceptions of their use of authoritative speech styles, which they felt were often negatively evaluated by both male and female colleagues. The female leader in my sample who commented that 'some men find me scary', was actually surprised at this reaction because she considered herself to be 'very approachable'. While three women commented that they were viewed as 'scary', not one man in my sample used this epithet, or indeed, commented on whether they were ever judged as such.

To *pre-empt* negative evaluation, these female leaders have devised a whole range of strategies, such as *warmth of manner*. Another leader describes the use of this strategy to regulate her manner when she speaks authoritatively:

> (2) You have to be prepared to make your point and stand your ground, even if you are being attacked. It's important at the same time to try and be warm rather than cold and hostile when you are being assertive in this way ... I think one should always be assertive in a nice way. I would say that being assertive is still not considered an acceptable form of behaviour, especially for a woman.
>
> (Technical SVP, space science company)

A second *pre-emptive* strategy is *humour*, already noted for its 'effectiveness' for conducting female leadership by language and gender scholars such as Holmes and Marra (2004) and Schnurr (2008). Humour is often used as a strategy to mitigate or soften the effect of orders or instructions, in order not to appear too authoritative or assertive. The following leader's references to her own language use indicate the constant imperative for a senior woman to 'police' her own language and to negotiate her linguistic relationship with others:

(3) I don't like sarcasm but I use humour softly. I can send myself up or be very self-deprecating. I can use it that way by downplaying my own authority to a certain extent. I can give orders but couch them in humour so that the effect isn't so threatening.

(Human Resources SVP, multi-national company)

Closely related to the strategy of using humour is that of *playing along with male colleagues* in terms of their humour and gendered assumptions. Another leader in the sample invokes the masculinist cultural prejudice against women in authority through her appropriated use of the 'sexist' term 'bully' (see Chapter 2), when she assesses the complex ways in which she is perceived and judged by an all-male Executive Board:

(4) I have a very good relationship with Exco ['executive committee'] and more than two of them will say, 'R. will bully us!' Me, bully them when they are two levels ahead of me! I think it is quite an affectionate form of teasing. I think they have given me permission to bully them and they tease me for it.

(Vice President for Global Diversity, multi-national company)

The use of the term 'bully', normally associated with men, has an exaggerating effect when used to describe a woman, as the popular American idiom 'bully broad' (with its conflicting sexist innuendo) also demonstrates. Here it is clearly used ironically by this female leader's male colleagues as a form of teasing, and has also been accepted by her ironically. But the fact that it has to be accepted rather than contested indicates the degree of linguistic self-regulation that many senior women must exercise. It is a *survival* rather than a *thriving* strategy because to contest this sexist practice would almost certainly jeopardise the approval this leader has won from her superiors, which is undoubtedly essential to her future success.

A fourth pre-emptive strategy women use to counter negative evaluation is that of *politeness* and sensitivity to the needs of others. This

involves senior women paying a greater awareness than male colleagues may have to pay, to the 'face needs' (Brown and Levinson
1987) of people on grades below them. While both male and female
leaders in my sample feel that a culture of politeness has replaced
old-style command and control leadership in most modern organisations, there appears to be an added pressure on female leaders to be
seen to be 'doing politeness' in a very evident way. The average female
leader under pressure may be instinctively no more polite than the
equivalent male leader, but if they fail to demonstrate politeness in
contexts where it is usually expected, the penalties may be more severe
for women (Brewis 2001). In the following example, a leader comments on the ways in which the cultural prejudice against women
'doing authority' continuously places senior women in a defensive and
vulnerable position, not least with their own sex. Here this manager's
guilty awareness of how she is viewed by her Personal Assistant ('PA')
is dramatised and therefore relived in all its painful detail, through
the reporting of her apologies and excuses. However, it is her evalua-
tive comments about how she tries to adjust her linguistic behaviour
(italicised in the extract below) that are just as telling:

(5) It [a direct order] *slipped out* this morning when I was rushing. I
said to my PA, 'chuck this one on right now, please', and she said
'when?' and I said, 'right now'. And then I went back and said, 'I'm
sorry, I've upset you but I did really need to get that out right now.'
When I have time it is more along the lines of 'this is what we need to
do, it would really help me if you do this'.
              (Human Resources SVP, multi-national company)

Both the use of 'it slipped out' and 'when I have time…' indicate
a certain level of conscious performance needed by this female manager, which involves monitoring her language so that it is sensitively
adjusted to the 'face needs' of her subordinates. It was clear that a
number of the female interviewees felt uncomfortable with giving
orders and instructions to subordinates, and have devised various
strategies to do authority without causing resentment.

A related pre-emptive strategy used by senior women to counter
negative evaluation from colleagues is the use of *mitigated (or softened) commands*, marked by politeness, hedges and the use of the
question form ('please could you just…?'). It is interesting in the fol-

lowing comment that the interviewee is quite explicit in gendering this strategy (italicised):

> (6) It's important to give orders and instructions clearly…this is what we need to get done and this is how we get there. *And this is a very female thing*, 'it would be good if you could do this for me'. I do not feel comfortable giving [direct commands]. I do it once in a while but the general theme is engagement versus ordering.
>
> (Marketing SVP, multi-national company)

Implied by this comment, the final pre-emptive strategy for dealing with colleagues that was mentioned by several senior women was *indirect engagement*. Several female leaders felt that it was often inappropriate to confront problematic issues directly (although they all said there were times when directness was essential). Sometimes it was expedient to 'bide one's time', however frustrating from a task-orientated business perspective this might prove to be. In the context of talking about a problem with a subordinate, this senior manager had the following to say:

> (7) [One of my team members] didn't want to admit to herself that she was having a difficulty but I knew you couldn't say, 'Oh you're having a difficulty'. I had to let her come to that conclusion. If that's a toolkit, that's the one I call upon. *I think it's a very male thing* just to power in and say, 'Are you OK? Are you sure?' And later when something goes wrong they'll say, 'But she said she was OK'. But you don't just make assumptions when someone says they're OK because it could rebound on you.
>
> (Human Resources SVP, multi-national company)

Again this leader explicitly genders the strategy (italicised) to distinguish her approach from her male colleagues. This strategy of indirect engagement shows this senior woman's awareness of the 'face needs' and deeper concerns of her subordinate colleague. She shows a number of 'relational' attributes: quiet reflection, patience, careful judgement and appropriately judged action, all of which take time and energy to perform effectively.

This and the other pre-emptive strategies mentioned above are indicators of the 'work' female leaders must do to monitor the way they speak compared to men. It is clear that they are partly pursuing such strategies to encourage good relationships with colleagues, but they are also doing this to further their own agendas as leaders. Their use of double-voiced discourse is motivated by a primary orientation to the self but is also regulated by the way they are perceived by colleagues, which triggers their use of pre-emptive strategies.

Is the use of double-voiced discourse in the interests of female leaders or not? The next section explores the implications of such linguistic strategies for senior women.

Discussion

According to the analysis of the interview data, female managers feel they need to be far more alert to the way their speech is evaluated than male managers need to be. In line with this, I suggest that senior women are often consciously operating a double-voiced discourse, one that constantly has to pay attention to other colleagues' point of view, while pursuing their own agenda. According to Bakhtin (1929/1981), the voice of 'the self' is thus enmeshed with and regulated by the voice of 'the other'. We saw in extracts 1 to 7 how female leaders use a range of strategies to regulate and shape the way they appear and sound to their colleagues, either to avoid negative judgement or simply to be viewed as more effective leaders. Among their pre-emptive linguistic strategies, women make use of:

- warmth of manner,
- humour,
- an acceptance of being teased,
- mitigated commands,
- forms of politeness and attention to 'face needs',
- indirect engagement.

From the research data it is clear that *all* business leaders are required to juggle between different and competing subject positions in order to achieve their business goals. However, female leaders arguably have the *added* challenge of having to perform a kind of 'interactional shit-work' (Fishman 1978) – that is, 'additional conversational work' to sustain a credible identity as a leader in order to avoid negative evaluation from colleagues. This assessment follows research in the same vein by Holmes and Stubbe (2003), which argues that while both males and females engage in 'relational practices' as leaders, these are still viewed as 'gendered' work and specifically associated with 'feminine behaviour'. It also follows research by Litosseliti (2006b: 49), which found that in analyses of argumentative interactions in the media and in focus groups, women are involved in additional conversational work to repair the effects of being typecast as emotional and hysterical, indeed as 'irrational females'.

The implication of these various research studies is that female leaders not only need to work harder to use language appropriately, but they need to be *expert* in the use of pre-emptive linguistic strategies in order to apply the use of double-voiced discourse effectively to thrive in their organisations. So, is the use of double-voiced discourse in the interests of female leaders or not? This expertise might be viewed as a *positive* feature because women must become more professionally attuned, reflective and linguistically dextrous than their equivalent male colleagues, an additional skill set which may give them an advantage over their peers. On the other hand, this expertise brings an added expectation for senior women to be 'superwomen' in order to cope with the rigours of senior leadership. Not only must they be intellectually and interpersonally effective but linguistic experts as well! While it is undeniable that certain women have reached their senior positions in companies because they *are* exceptional (Chase 1988), many perfectly able women may find the additional linguistic work required of them to be stressful, time-consuming and ultimately demoralising (Baxter 2008). Part of the reason for this, as Sheldon (1992: 100) argues, is that the message of 'double-voiced discourse' is 'harder to hear'. In other words, by mediating what you want to say through humour, politeness, tact, and so on, your message may get partially diluted, distorted or lost. This means that a woman's carefully nuanced comment may not stand out as much as if she had used the direct expression of single-voiced discourse. So the extra efforts of senior women to achieve a finely grained style of linguistic interaction may not necessarily win them greater recognition and approval at the top.

The value of double-voiced discourse to senior women must also be judged in relation to the gendered nature of the community of practice and type of corporation to which a leader belongs. In the Male-Dominated corporation double-voiced discourse is an *essential* mechanism for a woman to use for her survival. Hegemonic gendered discourses that negatively evaluate women as irrational, incompetent, bossy and bitchy are likely to circulate within this type of corporation. Here senior women are continuously negotiating 'the double bind' (Lakoff 1975): if they appear overly 'girly' or feminine, they may be stereotyped as 'a nice person' but also as weak, incompetent and lacking the required toughness for a senior job. If they appear overly assertive or confrontational, they will be characterised as 'scary', and regarded by their male colleagues as a threat on personal and professional grounds. In either case, such women run the strong risk of being sidelined or tokenised (Kanter 1977). However by using double-voiced discourse through pre-emptive strategies like humour, politeness, warmth of manner and so on, senior women can produce an impression of 'gender neutrality', which offers them an approved and credible identity in the male-dominated organisation. However, women operating with double-voiced discourses will never fundamentally challenge patriarchal values within the corporation, merely allow them to endure.

In the Gender-Divided organisation, senior women can appropriate double-voiced discourse in the cause of feminised values. Here there is a constant need to challenge the negativity of gendered discourses, and replace them with a positive evaluation of the attributes of female leaders. In line with the views of Helgesen (1990), Rosener (1990) and others, workplaces can benefit from the civilising effects of feminised leadership values such as openness, sensitivity to the needs of others and encouraging a sense of self-worth. Here, double-voiced discourse provides an effective set of strategies for female leaders to use to distinguish their approach from men, and to lead by example. Strategies such as politeness shows attentiveness to the needs of others, and humour provides a means of defusing tensions and conflict. Double-voiced discourse is less a survival strategy and more an essential toolkit for female leaders to thrive through *difference* within their organisations. However, double-voiced discourse is likely to *reinforce* rather than challenge gendered inequalities in the organisation in terms of perceptions of ability, distribution of roles and promotion prospects. This is because 'relational practices' are still viewed as 'gendered work' (Holmes and Stubbe 2003), and therefore the province of women.

Finally, in the Gender-Multiple corporation, both senior men and women will appropriate double-voiced discourse as part of the overall 'skills set' of an effective leader. Since transactional and relational goals are equally valued in the organisation, and indeed tend to support each other rather than being seen as polarised, the need for the voice of 'the other' to *motivate* and *inspire* the voice of 'the self', is a constant quest. As the Gender-Multiple corporation tends to challenge gendered discourses that negatively characterise senior women as incompetent, mean, bossy, irrational or whatever, senior women are under far less pressure to regulate their linguistic inter-actions with colleagues. Thus double-voiced discourse becomes a form of wise management, and part of the training and develop-ment of those heading for the top. It encourages a form of *self-reflexivity* within leaders – a capacity to shift constantly between action and reflection to produce a multi-faceted leadership style. It encourages the dual pragmatic goals of achieving sound relations with colleagues while getting business done effectively.

This chapter has shown how women have had to lead the way in using their linguistic expertise to be effective as managers. Some-times this takes the form of extra 'work' in using linguistic strategies to pre-empt negative evaluation, which can be very pressurising and perhaps demoralising. However, within the hospitable environment of the Gender-Multiple corporation, linguistic expertise offers a way forward for effective leadership. In the next chapter, I review a second case study which examines the actual *performance* of female leaders in senior management meetings. I explore the interactional strategies female leaders can use in order to be influential and effec-tive with their colleagues.

6
Case Study 2: Language of Female Leadership in Action

Introduction

This case study seeks to address the two principal aims in this book. The *first* is to find out whether there *is* a language of leadership that is exclusive to women, and the *second* is to explore how female leaders can utilise language as effectively as possible to achieve their business goals, and in certain contexts, to counter negative evaluations made against them because they are women.

Case Study 2 explores how one female managing director of the UK division in a large multi-national company uses an effective language of leadership to chair and run a two-day senior management meeting. Like many senior women who have survived and thrived in large companies, she is an exceptional woman. While in many ways she might be regarded as a role model in terms of her effective use of linguistic strategies, I am not presenting her as an absolute ideal; like everyone, she has her own style, and like everyone she makes errors of judgement as we shall see. Not all readers will like the way that she uses language to enact leadership. However, I will argue that she manifests the range of skills, strategies and aptitudes that have allowed her to be viewed as a 'high flyer', and on a fast track for promotion, within a top multi-national company.

The company in this case study is a highly profitable manufacturing business with a presence in over 50 countries. It takes pride in investing money in its people, and has a much higher than average employment of women and ethnic minorities at senior levels. The promotion of people to the top jobs appears to be less a case of

gender, and much more a case of whether a senior person is prepared to move freely from one country to another, and to travel, a
demand that of course may work against the employment of senior
women if they have traditional family commitments. People in this
company consider themselves to be well paid and their diverse
talents are recognised and rewarded. There are established promotion tracks and people can move quickly upwards through the
organisation if they have the required talent, flexibility and energy.
A rich international mix of relatively young people is found in senior
positions here. In my interviews with a number of the senior team
in the UK division, male and female managers expressed high levels
of satisfaction with the company describing it as 'having drawbacks
like anywhere' but generally 'a great place to work'. To this extent,
I consider that the company has many elements of the Gender-
Multiple corporation (see Chapter 4).

Like the previous case study, this study is broadly conducted from
a discourse perspective, which takes the view that leadership identities
(how people 'do' leadership) constantly interact with institutional
discourses, including discourses on gender. This interaction or 'dialogic' process (Bakhtin 1929/1981) helps to define roles, relationships, procedures, practices, attitudes, norms and values within the
corporation.

Map of the chapter

Following the Methodology section below, the rest of the chapter is
divided into the following four sections in order to present the
findings on how one particular senior woman ('Jan'), enacts leadership with her team:

(1) *Chairing skills*: this considers how Jan effectively deploys a
    range of chairing skills to steer her team of nine senior man-
    agers through a detailed and lengthy agenda.
(2) *Enacting authority:* this examines how Jan expertly enacts her
    authority as a leader, deploying a wide repertoire of linguistic
    strategies from a light touch to strong control.
(3) *Managing female subordinates*: this looks at Jan's strengths and
    limitations in managing a female member of her team and
    asks to what extent this is a gendered practice, and whether

this is an area where senior women sometimes fall short. Good working relationships between women could be essential in promoting the successful development of young, female, aspiring managers and leaders (Singh, Vinnicombe and James 2006).

(4) *Interacting with discourses:* this considers how competing institutional and gendered discourses interact with leadership styles to produce both effective and ineffective interactions within this corporation, which can work to support or undermine the authority and talent of senior women. One of these is the gendered discourse of *female emotionality* (Mullany 2007), which is seen to work against Jan as an effective leader in the data we examine.

Methodology

The case study represents the *second* stage of a larger-scale study of leadership discourse in business meetings. As described in Chapter 5, the first stage, aimed at eliciting senior people's perceptions of their leadership identities, involved conducting audio-recorded interviews with 20 business leaders from UK multi-national companies, ten of whom were female and ten of whom were male. The *second* stage, learning about the linguistic construction of leadership through actual performance, was to observe and record a series of business meetings. So in *this* chapter, the case study focuses on the practices of one particular female managing director chairing a strategic business meeting ('the Monthly Business Review').

The meeting took place off-site, in a hotel conference facility, over a period of two days, starting promptly at 9.00am and ending each day at 5.30pm. Items on the agenda included a review of the stock position of the company's products, a financial overview, pricing strategies, communication issues, career planning, and reward and recognition of staff. This key management meeting involved all seven members of the senior team which comprised the following (with pseudonyms):

- a female managing director (Jan)
- a male head of distribution (Michael)
- a male head of marketing (Francois)

- a male finance director (Simon)
- a female head of the legal function (Iris)
- a female head of human resources (Liz)
- a male country manager for Ireland reporting to the UK Division (Tim)

While the role divisions are admittedly a little gender-stereotypical, there was a diverse range of ethnicities reflected in the team: Irish, British, French, German, South African and Hungarian.

During this meeting, I was present as a complete observer (Gold 1958), sitting unobtrusively in the corner of the room. While my presence may have been evident initially, I was relatively confident that after the first hour or so, I was no longer noticed! The transcript data was gathered by means of two digital audio-recorders that were placed discreetly at either end of the boardroom table. They were switched on at the start of each section of the meeting and switched off at each break, and at the end of each day. I transcribed all the recorded data myself according to Conversation Analysis transcription conventions (Jefferson 2004; see Appendix 1).

In relation to selecting the extracts I present in this chapter for analysis, I opted for 'judgement' rather than 'random' selection of extracts for closer analysis and discussion (Mesthrie 2000). In line with a qualitative approach to analysis, an extract of data is studied for the richness of insights it delivers rather than its typicality from which generalisations can be made (Hammersley and Atkinson 1995). Thus, I chose sequences of linguistic interaction that on first impression appeared interesting or distinctive, and on second impression, offered a heightened sense of the overall character of the interaction. While a discourse analyst would choose to analyse any section of data and find it interesting (Cameron 2001), there are sequences within the data where the exchange is more intense, more engaged, and more focused. These sequences tended to encapsulate agreements, conflicts and shifts of subject position within the management team in clear, demonstrable ways, and it is these richer extracts that I have chosen to analyse in this chapter.

In terms of the analysis of the data, I used a range of methods to meet my varying purposes. For *Chairing skills,* I used the generic model of meetings devised by Bargiela-Chiappini and Harris (1997), as well an Interactional Sociolinguistic (IS) model of linguistic analysis which has been adapted to analyse business meetings (see Holmes 2006). This model analyses in very close detail the language used from one conversational turn to the next, paying attention to grammatical, lexical, prosodic and paralinguistic choices of language use. This method helps to understand exactly how different team members achieve turns in the discussion, and is especially useful for revealing differences between people's speech styles as well as differences in status and power relations.

For *Enacting authority*, I used speech-act theory (Austin 1962; Searle 1969), a method of linguistic analysis which identifies the form of particular speech acts such as commands, warnings, criticisms, and so on, in order to analyse how these achieve particular business functions. For example, a chairperson might use a question such as 'what's the time?' as a command in order to get a group to make a decision more rapidly. This seemed a good method to capture the pragmatic functions of leadership language: that is, how language achieves particular outcomes such as an instruction or a decision.

For *Managing female subordinates*, I again drew upon the IS model of analysing spoken discourse because of the way it can reveal the fine detail of linguistic interactions. For the final section, *Interacting with discourses*, I utilised a discourse approach to linguistic analysis (Baxter 2003), which looks at the data on a 'discoursal' level. The discourse approach aims to identify institutional discourses and to show how they work to 'position' individual speakers as they speak in competing yet related ways. For example, I identified patterns of language use which signified 'business focused' discourses, 'team-focused' discourses and evidence of alternative or 'interwoven' discourses. I also identified 'gendered' discourses, drawing on the evidence of previous studies as a means to label them (Mullany 2007; Sunderland 2004). This identification of discourses at a macro-level emerged inductively from the process of conducting the IS analysis on the micro-level.

I now discuss how Jan, the managing director (MD) of the team, uses these four aspects of leadership language to enact her leadership, and I also evaluate to what extent she is effective.

Chairing skills

In line with Bargiela-Chiappini and Harris' (1997) argument that chairing and leading a team are two distinct if overlapping spheres of activity, I propose to separate the analysis of Jan's chairing from her leading skills. An individual who is *not* the leader of a team may be asked to chair that team, either because s/he has a particular respons-ibility or area of expertise, or because the chairing role is appor-tioned on a rotational/democratic basis among different members of a team. Provided the appointed person understands the chairing role and its associated activities, s/he is in principle as capable as anyone else in taking the Chair; the rank of the individual in the organisation may or may not be relevant. Equally, a leader of a senior management team is likely to chair meetings with their own team, as in this particular case, and the activities of chairing and leader-ship may partially merge. It can be a challenging and sophisticated skill to negotiate the role of chairing and leadership in such a way that a meeting is well chaired, yet a leader's transactional and rela-tional goals are also achieved, as we shall see.

Tracy and Dimmock (2004) suggest that business meetings are explicitly task-orientated and decision-making encounters, involv-ing the co-operative effort of two parties, the Chair and the Group. While it is true that the focus is predominantly transactional requir-ing the achievement of specific business goals, Holmes (2006) argues that the chairing role must draw upon good 'relational practices' (Fletcher 1999) in order to achieve these business goals. She consid-ers that good relationships with members of the Group are essential if everyone is going to co-operate with the Chair and allow matters to be discussed, decisions to be reached, and actions to be decided. The balance between a predominantly transactional meeting and one which draws more upon relational practices may be influenced by its level of formality. Holmes and Stubbe (2003) comment that a more formal meeting will be large in size, have an explicitly structured agenda, formal procedures, specified participants and ritualised con-versational turns, whereas an informal meeting may be smaller in size, occur by chance, have a 'rolling' agenda, a relaxed conversational style and be open to anyone interested. As we shall see, Jan's meeting has elements of both, although a relaxed style pervades throughout and good 'relational practices' prove essential to its successful outcome.

According to generic models of meetings (Bargiela-Chiappini and Harris 1997), there are three phases of conventional activity: the *open-ing phase* which is chair-dominated and provides the interactants with context-setting, introduction of the agenda, etc, that is essential for their further engagement; the *debating phase* in which agenda items are discussed and resolved, the Group takes over more from the Chair, and various members are given tasks to undertake in preparation for the next meeting; and the *closing phase* in which the Chair regains control and final actions are summarised.

Because the skills required for each phase clearly change, I will consider Jan's linguistic performance as Chair in these three phases: Opening, Debating and Closing.

Opening phase

As this senior management meeting stretched over two days, it naturally divided into a series of 'sessions' on different agenda topics, because substantial breaks were needed for refreshment and a breather. Thus each new session comprised condensed features of the opening phase. Each time, Jan conducted very little in the way of formal preliminaries or context setting, but tended to 'plunge in' to the next agenda item. However, right at the start of the first day, she does 'context set' by outlining one of the key objectives of the meeting:

Extract 1:

(Small talk and banter around the table)

1 **Jan:** OK (.) shall we start? Um let's at the start of each session do what we said in
2 terms of saying what communications are out to the rest of the company in
3 terms of through the line (.) what goes into the news-letter (.) anything else we
4 said? what was the third one? newsletter? through the line?
5 **Tim:** team meetings wasn't it?
6 **Jan:** yeah (.) that's through the line (.)=
7 **Liz:** = through [the line
8 **Jan:**   [I thought there was a third? (2) I can't
9 remember (.) we'll see as we go anyway and phones on silent (.)

In this opening phase, Jan needs to interrupt the small talk and banter around the table, so rather than using an order to silence people, she uses an attention-gathering word ('okay') followed by a question. She then uses an indirect or mitigated command, phrased as a suggestion ('let's at the start of each session do...'). By line 3, she is inviting the participation of the team in her use of further short questions, which also offers suggestions of the kinds of answers she is expecting ('Newsletter? Through the line?'). Her open, participative approach works to a point. Tim contributes immediately with a suggestion, which is gently corrected by Jan, and echoed by another team member, Liz, as if in support of Jan's correction. Balanced with this inviting approach, is a sense of authority. In Jan's embedded command in line 9, 'and phones on silent', we have no doubt that the Chair is in control.

At the start of another session, Jan is more direct and business-like, setting the scene and being quite explicit about her objectives for this part of the meeting:

Extract 2:

1 **Jan:** right (.) the next thing on the agenda (.) what time are we? (2) ten to three (.)

2 the next thing on the agenda (.) we're running behind actually is 'rewards and

3 communication to the business' and I've put this on for discussion because we

4 talked about rewards last time and:: this is following the meeting on Friday

5 (.) what I want us to do is talk about what we want to communicate and who is

6 going to communicate to the business on behalf of the management team (.)

7 so who wants to start? (3)

In this opening, Jan reminds her team of the agenda, and the need to keep on time, so here she is explicitly performing her chairing function. Having given a more detailed setting of both the context and purpose, she then immediately invites people to participate, which signals the start of the debating phase. This is a direct, no-nonsense chairing style yet premised on team participation.

Debating phase

In this phase, Jan ranges between actively orchestrating the discussion to being just one of the participants. According to Bargiela-Chiappini and Harris (1997) the debating phase is largely characterised by group-to-group interactions rather than chair-to-group or group-to-chair interactions. Jan, because she is both the leader of the team as well as the chair, intervenes more than might be conventionally expected.

In the following extract, Jan, takes a 'hands-on' approach as Chair. A team member is giving a power point presentation, and Jan feels that other members are being insufficiently clear in their discussion of some figures shown on the screen, so she intervenes with a fairly directive question-answer approach in order that she, and others will fully comprehend a table comparing actual with forecast data:

Extract 3:

[*Note:* Lynx is a pseudonym for the title of a project. Some names have been abbreviated, e.g. 'Mic' for Michael]

1	Jan:	no (.) I don't understand that at all (2) so first of all overall company
2	Liz:	actual headcount
3	Jan:	actual headcount and company target after Lynx 2008 was 141.5?
4		*(Some conferring amongst team)*
5	Mic:	that's year end isn't it?
6	**Liz and others**:	yeah
7	Jan:	but that's what you need to be monitoring against, yep, the overall company
8	**Liz**:	but this is what....
9	Jan:	and while Simon is looking at that, what have you got for Lynx?
10	**Liz**:	and still we're trying to second guess, we've 9 versus 6
11	Jan:	what's 9 and what's 6?
12	**Liz**:	9 is the forecasted so we've allowed for extra bodies in Lynx by way of [um
13	Jan:	[and what's 6? 6 is target?
14	**Liz**:	yeah
15	Jan:	right OK

16 Fra: *(Indecipherable)*
17 Jan: let's come at it another way (.) Liz when you say
9 people who are the 9 people?

Here, Jan's leadership role appears to be overlapping with her chairing role, when she says in line 1, possibly on behalf of the group, 'No I don't understand'. This could mean that she is seeking a greater clarification on behalf of the meeting as Chair, but also that as MD, she is not 'getting' this important financial information. From that point on, she leads the questioning of Liz, briefly supported by Michael (line 5) in order to establish exactly what the figures are supposed to mean. Her questions are direct, goal-orientated and unsoftened by politeness strategies here. It is clear that she is acting as both the Chair and the leader of the team, in her almost instructional approach (line 17: 'let's come at it another way').

In other places during the debating phase, Jan drops back to become one of the members of the team allowing others to discuss points between themselves, and jointly producing the discussion on an equal basis with the others:

Extract 4:

[*Note*: Rory and Matt are pseudonyms for colleagues external to the team.]

1 Tim: Eddy =
2 Jan: = Ed[dy and Kevin
3 Tim: [Eddy and Kevin
4 Jan: yes (.) now Roy can go on that as well because he doesn't
have as much of complication=
5 Tim: =Aheee yes=
6 Mic: = no no (*Disagreeing noises*)
7 Tim: the FD they get nervous about it as well
8 Mic: yeah but maybe they are the minority just by being the
GM or FD they have
9   sufficient power to influence the [situation
10 Tim: [especially with a job
title like UK& I
11   Finance Di[rector
12 Liz: [yeah

13 Jan: yes OK (....) so Rory doesn't go on either so will you let
       Matt know that all
14   because I haven't er=
15 Tim: = yes:: it's all be::ing progressed(.) I think Kevin had a
16   meeting with that little fix-it guy from the company::'s
       office last week
17 Jan: OK
18 Tim: It should be done (.) might already have to be done last
       week

The collaborative and co-produced nature of this discussion is indicated linguistically by the use of agreement words ('yes', 'yeah', 'OK'), use of mirroring (Jan mirrors Tim and then Tim mirrors Jan in lines 1–3), and use of latching and overlaps, where people's turns are not quite completed before another speaker takes up a turn. There is only one brief moment of disagreement from Michael, who doesn't otherwise contribute. Jan is no different from the rest of the team in her use of agreement and co-produced features. Towards the end of this sequence (line 13) however, we do see Jan shifting from a position as just 'one of the team' to reasserting control as leader (rather than Chair) when she says to Tim, 'will you let Matt know that all because...' in order to give an instruction. Indeed during the course of the debating phase, Jan makes a number of skilled and nuanced shifts between three roles: from Chair to member of the group involved in co-constructing a discussion, to leader when instructions or orders have to be given.

Closing phase

I will now consider two examples of Jan's chairing in the closing phase, in which the Chair takes back the control and summarises the final actions, the first being quite exemplary, and the second being much more questionable.

The following closing phase is at the end of the first day of the two-day meeting, which has overrun by half an hour:

Extract 5:

1 Jan: so let's take stock (.) Rory is going to sit down with you
       Michael and Francois

2   to go through the legislation again to look at the different
         options is that right?
3 **Fra:**   we just cancelled the meeting with Matt
4 **Jan:**   (*mocking*) we just cancelled the meeting with Matt
5 **Liz:**   (*laughs*)
6 **Jan:**   (*jokily*) Matt is going to organise <u>another</u> meeting
7   (*loud laughter from whole group*)
8 **Jan:**   OK well I think that's it (.) any more on that item?
         (2) No? Sure? Well thank
9   you all very much (1) Michael are you joining us for
         dinner or rushing off?
10   (*Laughter and banter among whole group*)

Despite the late finish of this meeting, the tone of the closing phase
is good humoured, almost jocular, signified throughout by bursts of
laughter from the group. In line 1, Jan summarises her understanding of the action agreed by Michael and Francois – that a meeting
has been arranged with an outside colleague. This is instantly corrected by Francois who says that the proposed meeting has already
been cancelled by a more senior outsider, Matt. Rather than appearing annoyed that the Chair's action can't be achieved, Jan wields
her authority both as Chair and leader of the group by making a
light joke at the outsider's expense, thus ensuring in-group solidarity. Jan then signals the end of the meeting, perhaps a little
abruptly, but checks herself by inviting others to confirm that the
meeting should in fact end. She has anticipated their reactions correctly (line 8), so she thanks the team, and then looks ahead to the
evening's social arrangements, which effects a smooth transition
between business formalities and social informalities. The mood of the
group at the end of the meeting appears upbeat and harmonious.

   In the second extract, Jan's skills in chairing the closing phase
don't quite go to plan. Members of the group appear sullen and
unresponsive at the end of the meeting. What exactly goes wrong?

Extract 6:

1 **Tim:**   we ran out of steam we got to the roll-out to the Irish
         [market
2 **Jan:**   [no no we're not talking

3		about that (.) we're talking about the communication and the interaction
4		between the people around this table and the Irish business and the people in
5		the Irish business
6	Tim:	well yep
7	Jan:	yes? So that you need to come back and say exactly what you feel is best so we actually sit down and discuss it?
8	Tim:	yep fair point
9	Jan:	OK then alright so shall we have a break for five minutes is that a good idea?
10		it's like pulling teeth (*haha*) it's supposed to be the easy part of it (.) it's
11		supposed to be the nice part of it (*no reactions from rest of team*).

It isn't simply Jan's handling of the closing phase as Chair that is to blame for the sullen reactions from her team here. Negative reactions were set up right at the start of the opening phase of this same session, where she was too abrupt, perhaps abusing her impartial position as Chair:

Extract 7:

1	Jan:	the change management in the business has been <u>shite</u> so that's why I've put it
2		on the agenda to decide what we're going to communicate (.) how we're
3		going to communicate and who's going to do it (3) so I want us to be specific

The harsh judgement Jan makes of her team's performance in her role as their *leader* means that her *chairing* of the subsequent agenda item was bound to be a sensitive and challenging business. And so it proved. During this session, members of the team were quite confrontational with Jan, disagreeing with her judgement. In line 2, Extract 6, Jan's utterance 'no no', which interrupts her colleague, signals her clear disagreement with Tim's previous comment, which she then seeks to correct and revise. Tim seems willing to accept her correction in line 6, and Jan seeks quickly to check that agreement and build on it by asking a further affirming question about their new, tentatively shared position. Indeed, by using this affirmative approach in lines 7 and 8, Jan may have potentially rescued her position from appearing unfairly authoritarian. Her suggestion for a break may seem to be a good idea in order for all to 'defuse', but her use of humour ('it's like pulling teeth') goes down badly as only she laughs, and there is silence from the team. The use of humour can create solidarity as it did in the first example, but here it is perhaps perceived as yet another criticism of the team's 'shite' performance.

In summary, where Jan is able to make subtle distinctions between her role as Chair and as leader, she is largely successful in orchestrating the discussions in the group so that all feel they have a part to play. Where Jan's leadership role merges with her role as Chair so that the values of effective chairing such as impartiality and neutrality (Tracy and Dimmock 2004) appear undermined, Jan fails to gain group solidarity or their support of her as a Chair, which means she is in a weaker position to achieve the goals of the meeting.

Enacting authority

While chairing may be best conducted neutrally and impartially, leadership rarely can. As I have argued, the business of enacting authority continues to be more difficult for women than for men, if only because cultural discourses continue to endorse the notion that men rather than women are born and bred to be leaders (Olsson 2006; Still 2006). Enacting authority in key institutional locations such as meetings continues to be an extra challenge for women, even in Gender-Multiple corporations where women's power as leaders is better legitimised. I now consider to what extent Jan offers us a role model for her effective use of the language of leadership, despite the errors of judgement she makes at times. As introduced above, I will focus on her speech acts and analyse how these achieve particular leadership functions such as giving an instruction or making a decision.

One of the hallmarks of Jan's leadership language is that she deploys a wide range of strategies of enacting authority. These vary from direct and overt forms of directing her team, to more indirect and participative forms such as energising colleagues and encouraging team involvement. This is unlike the stereotypical male leader who may use a 'command and control' type model of authority (see Chapter 2), and is also unlike certain female leaders who may use co-operative, consensual and collegiate strategies predominantly (see Chapter 3).

First, while Jan is not afraid to exert her authority in obvious and assertive ways, she actually uses very few direct orders or commands. When imperatives *are* used, they tend to be deployed in a cautioning way (see (1) below) or offered as a suggestion (2) rather than expressed as a direct order:

(1) 'Be very careful that...'
(2) 'Everyone around the table, look at your own areas...'

When orders are issued, they tend to be softened either by the mitigated directive form 'let's' (3) or by the use of deontic modal verbs (words of obligation such as 'I want') in the form of a statement (4):

(3) '<u>Let's</u> not jump to conclusions'
    '<u>Let's</u> get that agreed...'
    '<u>Let's</u> get our assumptions right'

(4) 'I <u>want</u> this to be done by...'
    'I <u>need</u> this by next week'

Other ways in which Jan avoids the use of direct command is by the 'agentless passive' (5) (passive use of a verb which appears to have no subject). However as we see below, there is a risk that this use of language may be misunderstood because it is not clear who will be carrying out the order. It is also a hidden or masked form of authority on the part of the speaker, because it obscures the fact that it is Jan herself who is giving the order:

(5) 'Everything needs to be agreed'
    Instead of 'you will need to agree on this.'

(6) 'Let's have it all mapped out.'
    Instead of 'you will have to map it out'

Jan also moderates the force of many of her commands and orders to the team through the use of *voice*: that is, the first person singular, second person and first person plural, *I, you* and *we*. She shows that she can lessen or increase the sense of her direct authority over her team members through a change of voice. When Jan uses the *first person,* this makes the order or request seem very personal and very much her responsibility as a line manager. The use of first person is used sparingly by Jan perhaps because it can be viewed as too direct in some contexts and may cause resentment:

(7) '<u>I</u> want this to be done by...'
(8) '<u>I</u> need this by next week'

Jan uses second person 'you' in two senses. In the first sense, 'you' can be used *impersonally* to mean 'one', and therefore can sound inclusive (both 'I and you together'), which helps to build a sense of common experience between a leader and her team. In example (9), Jan is using 'you' in exactly this impersonal sense to include herself with her team. In the second sense, 'you' can also be used *personally* to mean 'you' as the object of an order /advice/ request. In this second sense, 'you' connotes a difference or separation between the speaker and her addressees. In example (10), Jan is separating herself from her team and thus implying that she is giving and they are receiving the order:

(9) '<u>You</u>'ve got to go in with your eyes open or <u>you</u> could get thoroughly shafted.'
(10) '<u>You</u> need to make sure that <u>you</u> don't get to the end of the year and find...'

Jan's most common use of voice is *first person plural* which implies a joint action expected of Jan and her team; this form of language assumes that 'we' are in this together: (this may not be the case of course, but it gives that impression!) When Jan wants to sound consensual, this is the verb form she tends to use, which softens the form of a directive:

(11)   'If <u>we</u> could get this done by late September that should put <u>us</u> ahead of the market'
       '<u>We</u> all need to challenge the Manchester team tomorrow'.

There are times when Jan misjudges the use of 'we', which sounded rather imperious on occasions, as if it were the use of the 'royal we'. Jan's self-awareness of this comes out in the following exchange:

(12)   Jan: 'Tomorrow <u>we</u> are all going to be challenging the Manchester team.'
       Tim: '<u>We</u> are going to be challenging the Manchester team?'
       Jan: 'The royal <u>we</u>!'

Jan makes use of a whole range of linguistic strategies in order to moderate the bluntness and directness of her authority over her team. Politeness in the traditional sense of 'politeness words' ('please, thank you, sorry') seems to be an essential element of her leadership language, often used to soften the force of a command (13). But also 'hedges' (words used to qualify or lessen the effect of a direct statement or command; underlined) are intrinsic to her style (14):

(13)   'Please would you take care of that, Tim?'
(14)   '<u>Perhaps</u> you could <u>just</u> get this out by...'

In addition to this more controlling if hedged style of language, Jan was also able to use a 'lighter touch', more collegiate, approach with the team, especially where she wanted decisions to *emerge* rather than to be imposed by her. In (15), Jan offers suggestions, in (16) she asks questions to invite team members to participate, and in (17) she asks questions to stimulate creative thinking in the team and to question preconceived assumptions:

(15)   'Why don't we consider going to Area and saying...'
(16)   'Would you like to add your views on that, Michael?'

(17) Let's turn the question around (.) why would we not want to present those? Are we not missing a trick here?

Although humour is not a strong characteristic of Jan's style, it is used to lighten the mood and encourage solidarity in the group, but rather than taking the form of set jokes or amusing stories, she tends to make flippant, ironic or throwaway comments:

(18) 'Let's not go there, let's not go there.'
(19) 'We're trying to be cool about it but really we're quite desperate.'

There are times in the language use of any leader, when the stress of the moment or a frustrating discussion creates acts of impatience, impoliteness, or even a possible abuse of their authority. It is difficult to judge exactly what marks this linguistically, because as I have argued in Chapter 3, language is multi-functional and defined by context rather than working in absolute terms (Holmes 2001). It is at times like these that many male and female leaders are open to possible criticism.

In (19), Jan's frustration with the discussion at that point is expressed by the use of impatience markers ('I don't care'); an explicit form of authority (because subordinates are prohibited from speaking in this way), which has the risk of causing resentment. In (20), there are examples of 'blocking' or directly controlling comments, reinforced by repetition ('hang on..hang on..'). And in (21), Jan uses short, sharp negative statements or judgements, and taboo language ('bloody') when she becomes particularly tense:

(19) 'I don't care who produces it, we just need something by...'
     'I don't care who does what from what department...'
(20) 'Hang on a second, hang on a second, hang on a second...'
     'Wait, I'm coming to that in a minute'
(21) 'No good'
     'I'm just not going to do it.'
     'You didn't do it right in the first place.'
     'I can't solve all your problems. You need a bloody good look at it.'

If a team of colleagues knows that a leader has a diverse range of linguistic strategies for enacting their authority, that team is more likely to forgive the odd, inappropriate or ill-judged comment. Indeed, a leader's propensity to be relatively direct when the occasion demands, and *not* to have to censor or police their use of language in order to pre-empt negative evaluation, may even incur respect from colleagues rather than opprobrium. But arguably, where women are concerned, there is always a 'downside'. The language of emotion, when used by women, continues to be associated with a 'discourse of irrationality' (Litosseliti 2006b; Mullany 2007), and may present a linguistic danger zone for women, while they remain 'on probation' as leaders. So there may be some potential restrictions to the wide repertoire of linguistic strategies that a female leader can use, but Jan shows that she is prepared to push the boundaries!

I now turn to the linguistic ways in which Jan enacts her authority in relation to a more junior female member of her team, as gender and leadership theorists have argued that good working relationships between women are essential in promoting the successful development of young, female, aspiring managers and leaders (Singh, Vinnicombe and James 2006).

Managing female subordinates

Perhaps one of the great, unspoken 'truths' within many organisations is that senior women may not be supporting junior women enough. Various language and gender scholars have identified a dominant gendered discourse in their research studies that seems to explain this phenomenon. For example, Mullany (2007) argues that the negative representation of senior women in the workplace as 'bitchy' is part of a greater gendered discourse on 'female irrationality' or emotionality (see Chapter 2), making them appear unsuitable for leadership. She argues that women's apparent tendency to 'bitch' about other women and sometimes men, means that they are viewed by male colleagues as not adopting a fair, impartial and reasoned stance in their working relationships with others. Sunderland (2004) identifies a 'women beware women' discourse, which normalises the assumption that women view other women as a threat, natural enemies, and competitors for the same male resources as potential partners and mates. Indeed, the 'women beware women' discourse is often seen in media texts such as advertisements, where older women look on jealously at younger women, who have carried off the prize of male attention. In a classroom study of all-female interaction (Baxter 2006), I noted how a group of 15-year old girls resented the way one particular girl opted to take the chairing and leadership role when conducting a discussion activity, and were unreservedly 'mean' (negative) when talking about her in individual interviews after the event. I argue that cultural expectations (Maltz and Borker 1982) place a pressure on girls to interact on an equal rather than a hierarchical basis, and to resist 'standing out' from the others:

> The female tendency to censure their own sex for 'standing out' is proposed as one reason why females sometimes find it hard to adopt authoritative or leadership positions in later life.
>
> (Baxter 2006c: 176)

In my view, the 'women beware women' discourse serves hegemonic corporate interests in providing common-sense reasons not to promote women to senior positions. However, in the Gender-Multiple corporation, gender is not seen as such a critical defining feature as it would be in more explicitly gendered corporations (Male-Dominated; Gender-Divided). In the Gender-Multiple corporation, the focus tends to be more upon a person's performance in terms of their previous career experience, educational background, social skills, readiness to network and to travel, and so on, as upon their gender or other social categories. Nonetheless, gendered discourses circulate within all organisations including the Gender-Multiple, although my own research experience suggests that they are more likely to be contested in this context as we shall see.

This section of the case study will explore two episodes in the meeting where Jan interacts with one of the two junior women present at the meeting. Again using Interactional Sociolinguistic (IS) analysis in order to uncover the fine detail of linguistic interactions, I will consider to what extent Jan supports, encourages and promotes the interests of her more junior colleague, and to what extent she (perhaps unintentionally) undermines her. As mentioned earlier, there are actually *two* junior women present in this meeting, Liz (the Human Resources manager) and Iris (Public Relations). I was interested to note that while Liz is fairly vocal throughout the two days, Iris says virtually nothing. This is compounded by the fact that Iris was assigned the secretarial role of taking the Minutes, and Jan never asks her to comment. Iris is therefore a silent woman, a phenomenon that is beyond the scope of this study to explore further (but see Jule (2006) on why some women choose to remain silent in institutional contexts).

I will consider two interactions between Jan and the more voluble of her two female colleagues, Liz. The first examines an interaction which appears to have a *negative* impact on Liz's ability to function effectively in the meeting, and the second is an interaction which has a much more *positive* impact. In the extract below, Liz contributes for the first time to this first session of the meeting (Day 1; 9.30am). What is interesting about Liz's intervention is that she introduces a *new* aspect to the agenda item under discussion, which is about the setting up of a new stratum of management at 'Area' level, which would have authority over the team:

[*Note:* Ian is the Area Director, Jan's line boss.]

1 **Liz:** can I just ask a question out of curiosity?
2 **Jan:** yep.
3 **Liz:** I know you met (.) with Ian and others around the table with Ian last last week
4   and the basis of (.) the decisions on (.) D. brand (.) but what has changed
5   (*laughs*) (1) in terms of the Area::?
6 **Jan:** what has changed (.) [nothing's-
7 **Tim:**   [Wh-what you mean?
8 **Liz:** no: it sounds as if like the old channels of communication erm I mean I know
9   the relationship isn't as good as all that but it's still the way it was compared
10   with the Area so I mean I'm not saying it should or it shouldn't it just [strikes me
11 **Fra:** (*Laughing as Liz speaks*) [it's just inefficient that's all
12 **Jan:** it's just it's just getting Ian on his own
13 **Tim:** without luggage in between him so we can have a conversation directly with
14   the Big Man himself.

15 **Jan:**   the whole purpose of it was to get Ian onside so we
         could talk about what we wanted to do with the
         busi[nesses
16 **Liz:**   [but they don't know that
17 **Jan:**   sorry?
18 **Liz:**   they don't know that
19 **Jan:**   they know it now
20 **Liz:**   they know it now

Here, Liz's metalinguistic comment ('Can I just ask a question out
of curiosity?') prepares her colleagues for her introduction of a
new angle on the discussion. Liz's laughter at line 5 and her use of
repeated pausing (.) signals her uncertainty about taking the discussion in a new direction, even though Jan as Chair has agreed to
her request, and granted her access to the 'floor' (line 2). Jan echoes
Liz's question in a mirroring comment ('what has changed? Nothing') but the answer is abrupt, and framed in the negative. Jan's
mirroring here is not a supportive sharing of a point of view, but a
repetition in order to dismiss. This isn't helped by Tim's lack of
comprehension of Liz's point at line 7 ('wh-what do you mean?').
Liz realises that neither colleague has understood her fully so she
attempts to re-articulate her point in lines 8–10. Jan and two male
colleagues then attempt to make sense of Liz's point in a short
sequence of co-operatively produced dialogue – where they seem to
be speaking as one voice (lines 11 to 17). Liz once again interrupts her
senior colleague at line 16 with the adversative conjunction 'but',
which suggests an alternative point of view or a disagreement with the
previous comment. Jan signals her annoyance at being interrupted by
means of a possibly sarcastic use of the politeness marker 'sorry?',
which may imply that she hasn't heard Liz's comment because she
was being talked over. Liz repeats her point (line 18), and Jan immediately makes a riposte (line 19). Liz's echo of Jan's riposte ('they know
it now') shows that she has closed off her objections; she is back 'on
message' agreeing with her boss' line of reasoning.

Liz has chosen to make her first major contribution to the meeting
by making a 'big picture' comment rather than an innocuous point of
detail, which Jan doesn't appear to welcome openly, perhaps because
it has disrupted the flow of the previous discussion, or because it
has raised a potentially sensitive area that Jan has not considered

exploring herself. Arguably, meetings need to be shaken out of their complacent routines, and Liz attempts to do this. It is understandable why such an approach isn't welcomed, especially when it is 'out of the blue' and perhaps handled in a rather gauche way by Liz. But it is also the case that Jan fails to encourage this more critical contribution. Could Jan have done more to encourage Liz here? I think so, because the response Liz receives is potentially off-putting, and could inhibit her from contributing in such a critical spirit again.

In the second extract, Jan handles her junior colleague in a much more encouraging and supportive way:

1	Liz:	can I make a suggestion equally
2	Jan:	yeah
3	Liz:	um just in terms of would it be worthwhile to pull the senior managers
4		together so that we can finally meet up just to (.) if we can find a solution just
5		to (.) if that is the decision fine I mean as long as it is clear because we're just
6		creating more noise and there's a lack of understanding and they need to
7		understand where we're coming from rather than just pissing them off further
8	Jan:	OK good point no good point (.) do you want to do that then (.) I'm not around
9		you see
10	Liz:	no nor am I but I'm happy to put it together
11	Mic:	what is Liz saying (.) I'm sorry I don't understand
12	Jan:	what Liz is saying is in terms of getting us copied in all the mail (.) want to
13		do that for a month so that we actually understand what is going on in the
14		business because it is 3 months now and every single month there are a few
15		things coming up that are causing us issues OK so what I'm saying what Liz
16		is saying is if we just do it without explaining why to everybody then it'll be

17   Jesus Christ what's the management team doing...(*Jan continues*).

Interestingly, this extract begins in a parallel way to the first extract above, in that Liz, in order to initiate entry into a discussion in which she has taken relatively little part, uses the metalinguistic strategy, 'Can I make a suggestion equally?'. This heralds her wish to be attended to, and is arguably an index of a less confident public speaker. Again, Jan agrees to Liz's request, which grants her access to this competitive 'floor'. Liz then speaks at some length in an uninterrupted way (lines 3 to 7), but this time, Jan responds affirmatively and positively to her point. Again paralleling the first extract, one of the male team members fails to comprehend the point Liz is making and seeks clarification ('what is Liz saying (.) I'm sorry I don't understand'). Is this because Liz is thinking on a more conceptual level that her colleagues are not always able to follow? This time, however, Jan is more in harmony with Liz's thinking and actually becomes a mouthpiece for Liz to the rest of the team. This could be viewed as an ambiguous strategy of support. On one hand, it clearly signifies Jan's firm endorsement of her junior colleague's point, showing which 'side' Jan is on. On the other hand, it suggests that Liz is incapable of speaking for herself, and needs Jan's support as a kind of translator. However, this time Jan reveals quite a degree of subtlety in handling her supporting role. In lines 15–16, she adjusts her use of 'voice', moving from first person to third person to suggest that this is a shared perspective rather than a translated perspective that she has appropriated ('what I'm saying what Liz is saying is...'). As a consequence of this exchange, it is far more likely that the apparently less confident Liz will have felt affirmed by her contribution to the discussion, rather than feeling undermined or excluded.

Female leaders bear a responsibility to support and develop more junior female colleagues in the corporation, while the concept of female leadership is still on trial (Singh, Vinnicombe and James 2006). Language can play a huge part in how successfully or otherwise this particular initiative is achieved. The above examples show how easily a choice of linguistic strategy can either affirm or undermine less confident female colleagues.

So far this chapter has conducted a micro-linguistic analysis of the ways in which senior women enact their leadership within meetings.

We have seen how an effective language of leadership is partially an outcome of a person's use of diverse, skilful and versatile linguistic repertoires within specific contexts. But this is always mediated by and negotiated through the prevalent discourses within a particular community of practice, as I now demonstrate.

Interacting with discourses

As we have seen, scholars of women and leadership literature have identified the presence of two dominant interactional styles shaping perceptions of leadership language and style: transactional and relational (e.g. Fletcher 1999; Holmes 2006; Still 2006). Scholars have further noted the presence of culturally governed, gendered discourses in organisations such as *gender difference, female irrationality/emotionality* and *masculinisation* (Litosseliti 2006b; Mullany 2007; Sunderland 2004).

Research evidence suggests that the Gender-Multiple corporation tends *not* to privilege one form of institutional discourse over another, such as transactional or business-focused at the expense of relational or team-focused (Baxter 2008). Effective senior managers are not constrained by the value system of one institutional discourse or leadership style over another, but, according to Marra, Schnurr and Holmes (2006: 256) 'skilfully integrat[e] transactional and relational goals' according to contextual factors. Derrida's (1987) theory of deconstructionist analysis proposes that today's institutional discourses should not just be perceived as separate, distinct entities, often conceptualised in opposition to each other with one discourse regarded as superior to the other (such as transactional over relational, and so on). Of course, discourses can be seen as separate and at times competing entities, but they can also be seen as interwoven in complex ways – a case of *both/and* (Cooper 1989). So, relational, team-focused discourses are interrelated with transactional, business-focused discourses within many organisational contexts.

Within our case study, the linguistic analysis has so far revealed that the managing director, Jan shifts between direct and authoritarian styles of leadership and more indirect, participative styles of leadership in order to accomplish interwoven relational and transactional goals. However, what we have not yet considered is how Jan's interactional strategies are mediated and shaped by pervasive institutional discourses. Using a discourse approach to analysis, I will examine the role of three institutional discourses that I observed were influencing speech styles, roles and relationships during the course of the two-day meeting. In line with above, I shall name these:

- A *business-focused* discourse: achieving business and transactional goals
- A *team-focused* discourse: achieving good relationships and a sense of team
- A gendered discourse of *female emotionality*: a tendency to characterise women in power as ruled by emotion not reason (Litosseliti 2006b).

This third discourse is well documented in language and gender literature on business leadership and practice (Litosseliti 2006b; Mullany 2007; Sunderland 2004). However, it also emerged inductively from my analysis of the data above as a means by which Jan was evaluated negatively by her team at different points in the two-day meeting. It appeared to act as a potentially *prohibiting* force upon the full range of linguistic strategies and behaviours available to Jan. I consider it to be a defining influence on the ways in which women enact the language of leadership, however egalitarian or Gender-Multiple a corporation they belong to.

In relation to this discourse of female emotionality, I had an interesting conversation with one senior woman who 'headed up a country' in an international corporation during my interviews with a group of senior business leaders (see Chapter 5). This female leader was concerned about her mood shifts in running long meetings with her team:

I often find my natural style is constrained by the needs and sometimes the *neediness* of people in my team. I find myself doing all I can to be the perfect leader. Then every so often I just snap, and all the good intentions go out the window. Suddenly I've lost my patience, I make a decision in the face of opposition and I can see the visible shock on their faces. Sometimes that's very difficult to recover.

(Female SVP, international corporation)

In this case, the female leader feels she has *not* skilfully integrat[ed] transactional and relational goals (Marra, Schnurr and Holmes 2006:

256) in order to make the best decision because clearly, she has caused her team to react against her. Her behaviour could easily be accounted for on psychological grounds: it is pressuring having to chair and lead all-day meetings: people get tired, decisions do need to be made, and business imperatives have to be met. Leaders cannot be superwomen (or supermen) all the time. But rather than viewing this 'mood snap' as a natural psychological phenomenon for which a leader could possibly receive coaching, let's consider it as partly an effect of the gendered discourse of 'the irrational female' which may potentially shape and proscribe female leadership language and behaviour.

To explore this further, we will examine how the three discourses (*business-focused, team-focused, female emotionality*) work in separate yet interwoven ways to shape the experience of Jan as a leader and those of her colleagues. In the first extract, we see Jan 'losing her cool'. She learns in the meeting that because of an accounting error, her arm of the business has *gained* an extra £1.8 million in their budget that they are not entitled to, and this error has not been reported to the level above. It means that Jan's position as an effective leader may be under question by *her* bosses. She is keen to deal with this, by shifting the problem back to the department who made the mistake in the first place:

(Note: WIT is a pseudonym for a higher senior management level)

1 **Jan:** I don't agree because the guys did a financial forecast (.) they <u>fucked</u> it up (.)

2 they have to do it (.) it's as simple as that (.) and if I'm sitting in a WIT

3 meeting and I turn round and say 'ah yeah but I don't have time to do this' (.)

4 no (.) give me a break lads (.) you say to me you don't have time (.) sorry (.)

5 do it right in the first place and then we're alright (2) they didn't do it right

6 in the first place (1) otherwise we wouldn't have the 1.8 million

7 **Liz:** [I know that (....)

8 **Jan:** [I'm telling you we'll be in severe danger of losing that losing it after having

9   been to the Area two months ago (.) not good (.) not
        good (.) so it's not about
10   dressing it up for them or anything (.) they'll all big
        guys (.) just do it properly
11 Mic: I hear what you're saying (.) fine (.) but given the mood
        in the business at this
12   point in time
13 Jan: uh huh
14 Mic: I think that we need to be cautious on how we treat the
        people

In this extract, Jan reveals her frustration at a very threatening situation through her direct expression of her viewpoint (line 1: 'I don't agree...'); use of taboo language (line 1: 'they <u>fucked</u> it up'); accusation of others (line 6: 'they didn't do it right...'); and abrupt judgement of subordinates (line 9: 'not good, not good'). In contrast, Head of Trade, Michael in disagreeing with his boss, sounds relatively measured and urbane ('I hear what you're saying (.) fine (.) but given the mood in the business...'). He suggests that Jan's solution to the problem – to make the financial people own up and correct their mistake – would be poor leadership judgement. He reinforces this view in line 14, when he proffers the admonishing comment, 'we need to be cautious on how we treat people'.

In this sequence, Jan invokes a gendered discourse of *female emotionality*, which, when interwoven with a *business-focused* discourse, produces uneasy and critical reactions in her colleagues. Jan's language reveals that a certain amount of anger and frustration at her colleagues is informing her attempt to make a quick and clean decision to solve this business problem. Michael, her subordinate, takes the moral high ground by expressing a concern for 'the people', which in better circumstances, might be Jan's prerogative. Michael is (perhaps unintentionally) positioning Jan as an irrational female leader, who is acting on impulse, failing to sense the mood of 'the people' and not sufficiently taking broader relational goals into account. In effect, a *female emotionality* discourse is working against Jan's achievement of goals within both the *business-focused* and the *team-focused* discourses in this context. So Michael becomes the voice of reason, Jan the voice of emotion, which potentially makes her appear unreliable as a leader of people. This sequence shows exactly how gendered discourses such as *female emotionality* can be actively constructed through linguistic interactions, and becomes an outcome or effect of a group of speakers' regular use of language.

In the second extract, which occurs a few moments later in the meeting, we see Jan seeking to recover lost ground, and actively attempting to repair her perceived position as the 'irrational female leader' operating according to emotion not reason. The value of studying the process of linguistic interactions is that a speaker's position is never static, always potentially reparable, as we see here:

1 **Jan:**	all I see (.) sorry guys but all I see is Q2 is spare 1.8 million somewhere
2	and 300 or something grand somewhere else [....
3 **Others:**	[Err:: (*Simon is trying to interrupt*)
4 **Jan:**	[I don't see anything (.) I haven't
5	been shown anything else (.) I've seen nothing else (.) that's all I've seen and
6	all I've seen is I go to the WIT (.) ask for 2 and a half million (.) hope the <u>fuck</u>
7	nobody asks me how are you doing without the money so I make up some
8	story about rephrasing you know? For me that's reality (.) that's why we
9	need to see month on month and anyway it's good practice we need to be
10	doing it because: once we understand the figures month on month on this table
11	then we know what we are doing with the business (.) it's a hell of a long time
12	since I brought that regime in and it's important for all of us anyway (.)
13 **Liz:**	it's a decision
14 **Jan:**	it's decision-making (2) OK? I understand what you're saying it isn't that I'm
15	not listening or anything like that but I have to do what I see

Here Jan is initially expressing a certain amount of emotion, indexed through her use of taboo language (line 7: 'hope the fuck'; line 11:

'it's a hell of a long time'), her refusal to listen, and interruption of others at line 3. However, she is attempting to reframe her previous position as an irrational boss, first with the use of an apology (line 1: 'All I see (.) sorry guys is...'), followed by a summary of what is already known (lines 1–2). She aims to win support for her position by encouraging them to visualise the difficulty she will face from *her* seniors (line 6: 'I go to the WIT (.) ask for 2 and a half million...'); evaluating her difficult position in a rational way for her team (line 8: 'for me that's reality'), and developing her line of reasoning into a policy for the future, to show that something strategic has been learnt from the problem (line 11: 'it's a hell of a long time since I brought that regime and it's important for us anyway'). Her possible success in persuading the others to see her decision more sympathetically is signalled by Liz's fairly neutral response in line 13: 'it's a decision'. Jan reinforces this implied endorsement by mirroring the phrase and turning it into a comment about effective leadership. She explicitly refers to her desire as a leader to integrate transactional and relational goals of leadership in her comment in lines 14–15, 'I understand what you are saying (.) it's not that I'm not listening...'

In this final sequence, Jan's subject position moves pragmatically between *business-focused and team-focused* discourses, by drawing on a more relational leadership style in order to explain and justify an unpopular business decision. She chooses not to retract her earlier decision to make the financial people 'own' the problem, but tries to appropriate Michael's 'voice of reason' by attempting to justify her decision within the wider business context of strategic policy. In this sequence, Jan's linguistic behaviour, while clearly reactive rather than proactive, is more likely to *contest* rather than reinforce the gendered discourse of *female emotionality*. She provides a set of reasons for her business decision; she encourages her team to enter her world and experience her dilemma through visualisation; she uses the incident as a means to produce longer term policy, and she makes it apparent to her team that she knows how she might be perceived according to the interwoven discourses of *team-focus, business-focus* and *female emotionality*, when she says: 'I understand what you're saying it isn't that I'm not listening or anything like that but I have to do what I see'.

This chapter has analysed the various and mostly effective ways in which one senior woman has used the language of leadership to chair a two-day long meeting in order to enact her authority in often difficult circumstances, to manage a female subordinate, and to resist and overcome negative gendered discourses.

Does Jan's experience suggest that there is a distinctive female language of leadership? The answer is 'No' to the extent that both male and female leaders skilfully integrate transactional and relational goals according to contextual factors, as we have explored in other parts of the book. But in the end, perhaps the answer is 'yes'. If Jan's experience is anything to go by, then the language of female leadership is both a more proscribed and self-regulated version of men's, but in many ways a more linguistically expert, diverse and nuanced version, finely-tuned to colleagues and context. Does it have a transformational power, energising and inspiring colleagues to share an exciting vision of the future?

Perhaps not as yet, but in the next chapter, I consider how senior women can further capitalise on their expertise with language both to foster the principle of a Gender-Multiple corporation and to support the position of *all* women seeking successful careers in the business world.

7
How to Achieve an Effective Language of Leadership

Introduction

In this chapter, I draw upon emerging practice from the key research studies I have reviewed so far to suggest the strategies and contexts which might enable *individual* senior women to use language as effectively as possible to achieve their business goals. I further consider strategies which *corporations* can use to counter negative evaluations made against senior women.

I shall build on this emerging practice by proposing *new* ways in which both individuals and corporations can work together to produce a more inclusive and hospitable environment for female leaders. I will therefore consider:

- *Individual* strategies that senior women can use to become linguistically expert within different leadership contexts
- *Corporate* strategies that might be implemented to support this individual linguistic expertise across the organisation.

However multi-skilled, resilient and proactive the individual female leader may be, she will have to work very hard to prove her effectiveness if she is not supported at various levels by the corporation. Ideally, therefore, a dynamic *interaction* or iterative process between individual linguistic expertise and corporate policies is the best way forward.

Individual linguistic strategies

One of the most powerful strategies by which an individual female leader can utilise language effectively to achieve her goals, and where necessary, to counter negative evaluations made against her, is to become not just a role model, but a 'linguistic' role model to her junior colleagues.

The use of role models in the business world is already well established. A Catalyst and Opportunity Now (2000) survey of MBA students in the USA found that 87% of women and 77% of men had said that it was important or very important to feature women business leaders as role models. The problem then and now, as we saw earlier, is that there are very few women at board level, both in the UK and elsewhere. Of these senior women, very few were considered to be good role models because they were forming themselves into male moulds (Ely 1994), and they were therefore viewed as *un*likely to facilitate the careers of younger women. Indeed, in a study of how young, female managers use role models, Singh, Vinnicombe and James (2006) found that very few of their respondents cited senior business women as role models, either in their own company or from elsewhere. Rather, role models cited were often male business leaders, members of their family, friends, media celebrities, politicians and writers. How can we use this information about role models and stereotyping to formulate a linguistic strategy for effective female leadership?

My proposition is that if there is a lack of female role models (as opposed to mentors) at the top of organisations, then senior and indeed, more junior women, ought to consider *becoming role models themselves*. By learning to become 'linguistic role models', as well as emulating others who provide examples of good business practice, women will establish their position in the corporation, while helping to build up the longer term 'stock' of female role models. The importance of younger or more junior managers becoming role models themselves is highlighted in the comment of this respondent in Singh, Vinnicombe and James' (2006: 75) study:

I undertook a task for my boss and he sent a memo to his boss saying I had done it very well which was super. And when I had to get the help of a junior person, I tried to be as supportive of everything she did, and I thought it would be nice to have her affirmation, and so I repeated what my boss had done for me, but of course this was at a much lower level. And she was so thrilled that I had done that. And to see that working down, that was a nice experience for me. It was that feeling of understanding how to deal with people that I learnt, it was a bit managerial, how to lead them and to motivate them.

While much has been written (e.g. Gibson 2004; Shamir 1995; Shapiro, Haseltine and Rowe 1978) about the qualities that make a good role model such as: achieving a judicious work-life balance, being open, sociable and good-humoured, and having an ideological mission, there has been little guidance on the *linguistic* strategies that make an effective role model. In order to address this, I propose that an effective individual strategy makes use of language in the following three ways as shown in Figure 7.1:

Figure 7.1 Individual linguistic strategy: a model of effective leadership language

Thus, a 'linguistic role model' might seek to combine three key ways of using language into an effective leadership language: doing authority, doing politeness, and doing humour. I now examine how this would work in more detail.

Doing authority

We have already seen in Chapter 6 how a managing director, Jan negotiates her authority as a leader through language, deploying an extraordinary repertoire of skills from light touch to strong control. This is unlike the conventional male leader who tends to use a 'command and control' type model of authority (see Chapter 2), and is also unlike the stereotypical female leader who tends to use co-operative, consensual and collegiate strategies predominantly (see Chapter 3). This ability to use a *repertoire* of linguistic strategies to enact authority shows that a leader can be flexible, versatile, multi-skilled and highly sensitive to context or community of practice (Marra, Schnurr and Holmes 2006).

However, a second way for women to enact authority effectively is to *develop a public voice:* that is, to take opportunities to speak in public settings by giving a speech or a presentation, chair meetings, or participate in public venues such as company meetings, or workshop and training sessions. Giving yourself a linguistic visibility is a very important means of being noticed and recognised for the value of your opinions, and one principal way of achieving this is to 'speak out' (Cameron 2006; Mills 2006).

A third way for senior women to enact authority is by using leadership language in 'warm' and 'cold' ways. There is a place for both in a leader's 'linguistic repertoire' (Holmes 2006), but arguably, 'cold' strategies need more self-regulation by women leaders than by men. 'Cold' authority is all about role and rank, a command and control approach, which brooks no discussion and debate from subordinates. 'Cold' linguistic authority is used when it is necessary to establish clear boundaries and expectations: if there is a crisis, this kind of direct, instructional power can be particularly valuable. If a pilot has to land a plane in an emergency, they are not going to say 'please' or 'thank you', but will just fire off instructions as they have been trained. Cool, intellectual authority, such as giving instructions, decisively telling people what to do, or pointing out a misunderstanding or conceptual error, has a definite place within leadership. Arguably, this is more likely to win respect, if used appropriately, than a warmer, more oblique approach. But the 'cold' approach may also be a potentially risky strategy for women – if routinely used without warmth of manner (see Chapter 5).

'Warm' linguistic authority is debatably a far more effective means of negotiating authority with a team in the longer term. This is because it involves generating *energy* as a leader, encourages inclusion and engagement, and builds the collective motivation of the team. In this way, single-leader authority is partially dispersed and becomes collectively 'owned' by the team.

Doing politeness

Politeness is a fundamental way in which people engage in social and professional relationships (Brown and Levinson 1987). It involves both 'negative' face needs (allowing other people to go about their business without undue imposition), and 'positive' face needs (attending to people's needs for approval, appreciation and respect). As demonstrated in Jan's case in Chapter 6, politeness is an essential part of leadership language in that it helps to moderate the blatant imposition of authority upon subordinates, and to allow people to think that a leader's decisions are collaborative and jointly produced rather than coercive. It is an important way of constructing good team relationships by developing rapport and maintaining collegiality. This means that when team members challenge a leader's authority, they are more likely to express this in socially acceptable ways by using polite forms of address, hedging a statement, asking a question, or clarifying a point, rather than making a bald complaint or criticism.

Once again, it is possible to distinguish between 'warm' and 'cold' forms of politeness. 'Cold' politeness, signified by the use of a more formal, respectful language (for example, use of titles such as *Mr/Ms*, or politeness markers such as *please* and *thank you*) has its role in enabling female leaders to function effectively in certain more formal or ceremonial settings. Singh (2008) in her report of boardroom cultures, cites the example of Sir Peter Parker, chairman of the UK National Grid, who in his bid to encourage a more 'inclusive' Boardroom, never allows 'rough' or aggressive language to disrupt proceedings, and ensures that every director systematically gets their turn to speak. This way of 'doing politeness' can at times seem rather stiff, formal, perhaps 'phony' and even patronising, but there is no doubt that it is necessary in these larger forums as a linguistic way of enabling everyone's voice to be heard. Within the more informal context of team meetings, 'cold' politeness of this type might be used more circumspectly as it can distance people rather than bring them together in a collective enterprise. 'Warm' politeness, on the other hand, expresses a genuine interest in the other person, offers space to engage, and is a means of entering another person's world. It signifies that a leader values her colleagues' viewpoints, respects where they are 'coming from', and helps to garner the support of others for collective team action.

Authority and politeness are often interwoven with a finely judged use of humour in an effective leader's speech style, as I now discuss.

Doing humour

Humour is a valuable leadership resource in workplace interactions, and it has the ability to perform many functions (Schnurr 2008). Humour releases tension, reaffirms group solidarity when it has been tested or challenged, and provides vital breaks from the serious work of conducting business. Indeed, like small talk, humour often occurs within meetings, often at transition points (at the start of a meeting, between agenda items, towards the close), and often follows a difficult discussion. Unlike the linguistic strategies required for negotiating authority and politeness, humour is not easy to acquire as a learnt skill – some people appear to 'do' humour more 'naturally' than others, and humour has stereotypically been associated more with men (e.g. Coates 2004; Decker and Rotondo 2001; Schnurr 2008).

Nevertheless, humour can be regarded as an essential resource for conducting leadership as it typically constructs participants as equals (Holmes and Stubbe 2003), emphasising what they have in common and playing down power differences. It therefore interacts in complex and subtle ways with both enacting authority and politeness. In terms of *authority*, humour may be a useful strategy for lessening the impact of 'face-threatening acts' such as commands and criticisms that impose upon a person's freedom of action. It is also a more socially acceptable resource for subordinates who may wish to challenge or contest a leader's authority without being too direct (Decker and Rotondo 2001). In terms of doing *politeness*, humour can provide a 'cover' for a remark which might otherwise be deemed too bald, blunt, critical or personal in leadership contexts. Humour in this sense acts as a form of politeness.

Once again, we can distinguish between 'cold' and 'warm' humour, where 'cold' or 'negative' humour (Morreall 1991), may be a danger area for female leaders if they are not wholly accepted. 'Cold' humour typically aims to attack people personally and single out victims instead of creating common ground. It often includes ambiguous types of humour such as irony, sarcasm, and teasing to bully, which are not overtly funny and indeed, can hurt (Morreall 1991). 'Warm' or positive humour on the other hand, aims to foster good relationships by creating an open-minded atmosphere and a sense of 'in-group' identity (Tajfel 1978). This use of in-group identity is often pitted against a notional 'out-group' (another department, people on the grade above, difficult clients, rival companies). 'Warm' humour includes features such as anecdotes, wordplay, self-denigrating humour, and gentle teasing of one's colleagues (Schnurr 2008).

In sum, I propose that an effective female leader should aim to interweave all three linguistic strategies of enacting authority, politeness and humour to accomplish business and relational goals, and also to support the quest of acting as a role model to more junior female colleagues. Perhaps the real skill of a leader with linguistic expertise is to decide *in a split second* how to achieve the best blend of strategies for their audience, context and purpose. It may also be a matter of using 'double-voiced discourse' (Sheldon 1992) in its most positive sense: as a linguistic radar that makes fine discriminations about the kind of language to use in response to different colleagues and communities of practice.

How can the *corporation* help to support their female leaders as linguistic role models in the greater quest of producing a more hospitable, female-friendly environment in which women can thrive? An individual female leader will struggle as a linguistic role model if she is not also given strong institutional back-up.

Corporate linguistic strategies

There are already many examples of corporate good practice in developing inclusive, female-friendly boardrooms. For example, a report commissioned by the UK Resource Centre for Women in Science, Engineering and Technology (Singh 2008) identifies a number of widespread good practices already used by large, multi-national companies such as:

- recruiting more women and ethnic minorities in senior executive positions,
- induction programmes for new managers,
- considerate treatment of people in the boardroom,
- team-building exercises for the whole new team when new directors join,
- inclusive and structured succession planning,
- encouraging senior women to become role models to more junior women,
- developing those in the talent pool by including coaching and mentoring,
- flexible working arrangements for staff so that they can achieve an effective work-life balance, and
- developing an inclusive workplace culture spearheaded by the chief executive.

What is immediately striking however is that this list does not offer examples of *linguistic* practices, other than that implied by the third bullet point above ('considerate treatment of people in board-rooms'). This point is developed later in Singh's report (2008: 1) by recommending that meetings be conducted 'with courtesy, consideration and control so that business can be conducted in a courteous atmosphere that allows everyone to make their contribution' (Singh 2008: 1). So, the report does acknowledge to a degree that language has a role in retaining women in top positions. It suggests that the Chair must act as a senior role model in showcasing ways in which boardroom meetings are managed and led, in order to involve women and enable their voices to be heard.

However, organisations are 'missing a trick' if they fail to appreciate the wider *range* of linguistic strategies for achieving female-friendly boardrooms and more inclusive corporations. There may be good reasons for this linguistic omission. As Mills (2003) argues, one of the problems is that linguistic policies are often perceived to be quite abstract because they involve people's attitudes, and are therefore regarded as personally intrusive. Indeed if a company attempts to institutionalise a linguistic policy, it may be accused of taking a 'big brother' or 'thought police' stance, which is why so many such policies were discreetly dropped by businesses after the 1970s (Cameron 1995). While leaders can do much on an individual level to enhance their linguistic expertise, corporations have a much harder job to institutionalise inclusive language policies in acceptable ways.

One way in which corporations can help to support female leaders as linguistic role models but also develop an 'acceptable' corporate policy, might be to informally appoint people at different levels and in different functions to be 'linguistic champions'. Their role would be to help colleagues to develop a greater linguistic awareness, and to provide expertise and advice. Female leaders might opt to be linguistic champions, but this expert group should also comprise male and female staff from corporate affairs and human resources. I develop this idea further in the discussion that follows.

A second way in which corporations can help to support female leaders is by raising awareness of the effects of 'gendered discourses', which tend to evaluate senior women in negative and discriminatory ways (Sunderland 2004). In this book, I have explored different examples of gendered discourses such as *female emotionality* (Chapters 2 and 6); *gender difference* (Chapter 3); *masculinisation* (Chapter 4) and *women beware women* (Chapters 3 and 6). As seen in Singh's (2008) report above, many corporate policies do little to challenge gender discrimination in people's *attitudes*, often reflected in both public and particularly, private conversations. Those with a responsibility for linguistic expertise therefore need to recognise the forms that gendered discourses take in order to plan ways to encourage a more healthy diversity of discourses within the organisation. However, again this isn't about *countering* discriminatory attitudes in a 'thought police' kind of way; it is about *encouraging* a hospitable linguistic environment where multiple discourses on gender are invited, and free discussion and debate on these issues are welcomed.

I now investigate the different ways a corporate linguistic strategy can resolve discriminatory attitudes that may surface through gendered discourses. This can be achieved by contesting discourses in the following five areas: use of sexist language; terms to describe women; use of metaphors; generalisations; gossip and mean talk. In helping to address discriminatory attitudes, the corporation can enable senior women to use a language of leadership that is free of excessive self-regulation, and is therefore more potentially expressive of 'how they might wish to be': their preferred professional identities.

Contesting use of sexist language

One way in which the business world *has* successfully challenged discriminatory attitudes about women is by offering guidance on the use of so-called 'sexist language'. In the 1970s, there was a concerted attempt across many public institutions to support equal opportunities and sex discrimination legislation with equivalent language planning. Policy-makers aimed to intervene in the use of everyday language in order to replace 'sexist' language with inclusive language in the hope that people might think and act in more gender-inclusive ways. Hence, writers in education, the media, publishing and the business world were encouraged to change the way language was used in these contexts. Influenced by guidance such as Miller and Swift's (1981) *Handbook of Non-sexist Writing*, workplaces were urged, for example, to:

- Replace the generic pronoun *he* with *he/she* or the more derided *s/he*.
- Substitute the title *Ms* for the two existing titles *Miss/Mrs* for women
- Substitute gender-neutral, occupational terms such as *Chair* for *Chairman/woman* and *Manager* for *Manager/Manageress* in business and public contexts.

These gender-neutral terms had their desired effect in so far as people *talked* about them, but this in turn generated a satirical backlash against 'political correctness', which some argued was counterproductive for women.

None the less, this movement against anti-sexist language has largely been successful. Businesses found that if they were to employ talented women or people from ethnic minorities, the language and imagery of their publicity materials had to be more neutral and inclusive. Most western businesses have long since incorporated the principles of 'anti-sexist language' into diversity policies, which have more or less become a 'received wisdom'. Pauwels (1989) cites changes in naming practices, occupational terms and professional titles, generic

nouns and pronouns, which led to an avoidance of gender stereotyping in employment, advertising, administration, the media, education, as well as in linguistic texts such as dictionaries, grammars, and
government reports. Interestingly, this 'top-down' initiative continues
today. Recently, British newspapers such as *The Telegraph* (e.g. Johnson
2009) reported in satirical terms a European Union (EU) initiative
to ban the terms *Mrs* and *Miss* (along with *Frau/Fraulein, Madame/
Mademoiselle* and *Senora/Senorita*) in all EU countries, replacing them
with the equivalent of *Ms*.

I suggest that official policies about non-sexist language *have* helped
to raise awareness about the power of individual words to construct
longer term attitudes and prejudices against women. Today, it is a
matter of building on well-established diversity policies by cultivating
an awareness of the negative effects of linguistic stereotyping through
names, professional titles, and so on. This advisory approach would
also be appropriate for contesting negative terms to describe women,
which I consider in the next section.

Contesting use of terms to describe women

A second, more pertinent way in which a corporate linguistic strategy can challenge discriminatory attitudes is by raising awareness of
the terms used to describe senior women. In my interviews with
both senior women and men (Baxter 2008), as well as in previous
research (e.g. Olsson and Walker 2003), women leaders are routinely
described in unflattering and derogatory terms. They are described
as *hard, difficult, scary, tough, mean, bullying, assertive, aggressive,
volatile, overpowering, shrill, hysterical, emotional, moody* and *irrational,
lesbian, feminist, transvestite,* as illustrated in this senior woman's
observation:

> Some corporate women can be quite hard. We joke about them
> being corporate transvestites because they look like women but
> they dress and act like men.
>
> (Olsson and Walker 2003: 6)

These terms used by people in the organisation to describe
more powerful women are not words of innocent fun, but actually
contribute to discriminating practices. Again, I would argue that
any company edicts of a *'thou shalt not'* variety would be deeply

counter-productive. But raising an awareness of this issue within diversity policy literature or within leadership and team-building workshops might constitute an important way of challenging a casual yet potentially damaging use of language. While it is likely that such ways of describing people will crop up in casual conversations rather than in written documents, corporate affairs staff responsible for communications should develop linguistic expertise so that they are alert to gendered implications. A headline like 'the girls on the front desk' (as I saw in one company in-house magazine) might seem a chatty and engaging representation of these receptionists, but contrasted on the same page with the representation of a group of male staff as 'men with a mission', this expression serves to trivialise these women's jobs.

Contesting masculinised use of metaphors

A third way in which a corporate linguistic strategy can challenge discriminatory attitudes against senior women is by raising awareness of the use of metaphor. According to the cognitive linguist, Koller (2004: 9), the reason this is important is that 'metaphor is a conceptual phenomenon that is realised at the surface level of language'. In other words, metaphorical language manifests and helps to reproduce deeper social values, attitudes and in this case, prejudices.

Koller (2004) among others has noted that war/fighting metaphors are by far the most prevalent in business contexts, followed by sporting, games and mating metaphors. Specifically, she found that war and sports metaphors were routinely interrelated in reports of competition between big multi-nationals. In my own interviews with business leaders, (Baxter 2008: 211), I found that war and sporting metaphors were used in their talk as a means of conceptualising leadership, with one senior woman suggesting that in order to be effective 'you have to be prepared to make your point and *stand your ground*, even if you are *being attacked*' (my italics).

Koller (2004) is one of a number of researchers who argues that the way in which business language is constituted by war and sports metaphors helps to 'masculinise both that discourse and related social practices'. The kinds of masculinised attributes associated with business and leadership are exemplified in the frequent use of metaphors such as:

> Target, hostility, battle, war, defence, fight, raid, attack, victory, fierce, troops, prey, defeat, killer, arms, bruise, assault, blood, enemy, brutality, combat, victim.
>
> (Koller 2004: 214–215)

Since war can be considered a 'quintessentially masculine activity and an essential test of manhood' (Wilson 1992: 892), its metaphoric usage arguably helps to marginalise metaphoric femininity and consequently, position women as an 'out-group' in business. Repeated use of war metaphors, both in quantitative and qualitative terms thus 'strengthens...a predominantly male culture' (Wilson 1992: 898). In this sense, war (and sporting) metaphors serve an ideological function, and tend to reinforce a 'think leader, think male' culture. Therefore, the use of masculinised metaphors is one significant way in which gendered discourses are constructed, sustained and perpetuated through leadership and business language, and almost subliminally can make life for many women leaders an alienating experience. Indeed, Heilbrunn (1989: 18) argues that their use is far from being beneficial for men either, because it may bring about ethical problems in 'making it easier to accept behaviour – such as unchecked ruthlessness and brutality – otherwise considered to be problematic'.

But if metaphors work on such a subconscious level through culturally accepted idioms, is there any way in which a corporate strategy can contest such linguistic practices? Koller (2004) suggests that corporations should be prepared to coin *new* metaphors, but is this a step too far? In her analysis of metaphors in business publications, she argues that writers and journalists with a responsibility for communications should be trained in an awareness of masculinised metaphors and their power to shape social realities. Koller (*ibid*) suggests that organisations can build on pre-existing, less familiar yet routinely used metaphors such as *Markets involve conversation* or *Merging companies are developing organisms* (see Koller 2004: 177). Conscious use of such alternative metaphors in training venues and in-house publications might help to 'defamiliarise' the ways in which business practices are presented by:

> making the routine or ordinary seem strange or different by presenting it in a novel light, by placing it in an unexpected context or by articulating it in an unusual manner...metaphoric defamiliarisation thus provides epistemic access to alternative aspects of reality.
>
> (Walters-York 1996: 59)

Thus, within in-house publications, corporate affairs staff might consider exploring the use of alternative, non-violent, metaphors to describe business and leadership practices. In my interviews with business leaders (Baxter 2008), I found that a range of metaphors are used alongside war and sporting metaphors such as therapy, dance and even romantic or sexual love. These alternatives suggest that there are 'counter-discursive' ways of 'metaphorising' business and leadership practices. However, there is no doubt that this fundamental form of linguistic challenge is difficult to accomplish at corporate level without a clear human resources policy on language, and may incur people's resistance and ridicule. But perhaps resistance and ridicule is the first stage towards a more widespread linguistic awareness about the discriminatory effects on women of gendered discourses?

Contesting the use of generalisations

A fourth way in which a corporate linguistic strategy can challenge discriminatory attitudes against senior women is by raising awareness of the common use of *generalisations* about gender in people's conversations. Generalisations may seem harmless enough, but they are part of the linguistic expression of the gender difference discourse, which seeks to stereotype the apparent differences between male and female behaviour (Gray 2002; Tannen 1994). In casual conversation, it is common to hear people say such things as 'He's a typical man; he never listens to what I'm saying', or 'She's a woman; she lives on her emotions.' Such apparently harmless generalisations serve to reinforce social prejudices about what the sexes supposedly can or can't do.

The Catalyst and Opportunity Now report (2000) observed that stereotyping is perceived by leaders to be the biggest barrier to women's careers, creating narrow and limiting definitions and subject positions for female managers. Language is one of the primary ways by which stereotypes are constructed (though they are also sustained through other aspects such as appearance and behaviour). However, linguistic stereotyping is unlikely to be tackled successfully through heavy-handed diversity policies stating that generalisations are 'banned'. An alternative approach is to encourage people to be alert to stereotyping, so that it can become a principle guiding the good practice of interacting in the corporation. Those appointed as linguistic champions can routinely point out the *effects* of generalising others on the grounds of gender, ethnicity, and so on, in appropriate training contexts.

Perhaps the best form of 'awareness-raising' is through humour and irony, whereby those who are more linguistically aware can gently tease others who make sweeping yet damning generalisations. So if someone makes a throwaway comment such as 'Men are hopeless at expressing their feelings', a linguistic champion might counter, 'That's odd, Mike in IT is rather good at it!'. Constructing stereotypes often takes the form of humorous banter or witticisms, which is why a humorous response may be the best form of challenge. Some of the most pernicious stereotypes about race, ethnicity, disability, sexuality and gender are purveyed through 'negative' humour (Morreall 1991): that is, criticisms of people that are deemed to be comic. However, I do not underestimate how difficult it is for corporate strategy to 'tread a fine line' between tackling demeaning stereotypes and demonstrating a lightness of touch!

Contesting gossip and 'mean talk'

The last and perhaps most controversial way in which a corporate linguistic strategy can challenge discriminatory attitudes against senior women is by raising awareness of their role within gossip and mean talk.

Gossip continues to be a folklinguistic stereotype of the way *females* typically use informal language. On this basis, gossip was 'reclaimed' by early language and gender theorists as a vital way in which women manage private conversations in close, female relationships (Jones 1980). According to Jones, women's gossip, encompassing 'scandal' and 'bitching', is a 'language of intimacy...arising from the solidarity and identity of women as members of a social group with a pool of common experience' (1980: 244). Subsequently, some researchers have found that men gossip too, but follow a narrower definition of gossip – for example, as malicious talk about other people in their absence, often to assert their heterosexuality (Cameron 1997).

'Mean talk' is a phrase I coined from the film 'Mean Girls' (Paramount Pictures 2004), and is based on research I conducted on single-sex female talk in a comprehensive school in the UK (Baxter 2006c). I noticed that a group of 15 year-old girls used 'mean talk' against individual girls who tried to take on the role of leader, which seemed to be highly resented by the group. I deduced that girls find it difficult to accept a female leader in an all-female group because they are socialised into creating relationships of equality and trust (Maltz and Borker 1982). Because it is still regarded as socially unacceptable for women (unlike men) to tell each other what to do, or to confront each other in assertive and even aggressive ways, women are socialised into more passive and co-operative ways of accepting authority from each other or resolving conflicts. If women consequently have a difficulty in accepting one of their peers as a leader, this may partly account for the construction of a *women beware women* discourse in organisations. This discourse is more likely to be reproduced within informal, social talk rather than in public settings such as meetings, where 'mean talk' would be deemed professionally inappropriate. However, if women can't support each other, openly and actively in public, isn't it always going to be harder for women to make it to the top, and once there to sustain their position whilst not losing their female friends?

I proposed earlier that on an individual basis, talented senior and junior women might aim to be role models within their organisations. Language can play a huge part in how successfully or otherwise this particular initiative is achieved. The examples of interaction analysed in Chapter 6 show how a choice of linguistic strategy (such as supporting a contribution made by a more junior colleague in a meeting rather than abruptly 'putting it down') can positively affirm less experienced female colleagues.

But can there possibly be a *corporate* linguistic strategy designed to counter the possible negative effects of gossip and mean talk? While these forms of talk almost certainly serve a social purpose in giving women (and men) a private, non-aggressive channel by which to resolve tensions and conflicts, they can also serve to reproduce a *women beware women* gendered discourse, which does not serve female leaders' best interests. For the moment, I have just one suggestion for corporate policy, while recognising this to be a highly sensitive area of professional relationships. My reflections are therefore work-in-progress. As talented senior men and women progress through the organisation and apply for, or are identified for promotion, they gather a 'storage' of qualities, attributes, behaviours, characteristics, features that become strongly associated with them. Some of these features are seen as strengths, others as limitations. As Human Resources staff and senior colleagues consult about the talented person's eligibility for pro-motion, some of the stored comments circulate in the form of gossip, and mean talk will inevitably surface. My suggestion is that companies *formalise* this gossip and small talk by bringing these stories to the surface. So, 'this and this is said about the person...what do we think of this? Is there any evidence? How much does this matter? What is good about these stories, what less so? What are the implications for his/her career?'

Without proposing to *institutionalise* gossip and mean talk, those responsible for enabling promotion could make *more* of the stories that are told about a person, both the positive and celebratory as well as the negative and more malicious. By bringing the more negative stories to the surface, their slightly clandestine aspects are challenged, and any dubious aspects are questioned and submitted to scrutiny. By means of this process, some of the myths and stereotypes associated with talented senior women – as scary, tough, mean, volatile, difficult, hard-going, and so on, might be contested and overturned – on the basis of evidence.

8
The Linguistic Landscape of Female Leadership

In this final chapter, I shall give my response to the driving question of this book, 'Is language a reason why female leaders continue to be under-represented at senior level?' This book has shown how a senior woman's use of language has constructed a leadership style that at times contrasts uncomfortably with the masculinised norms of the business world (Vinnicombe and Singh 2002). A contrast in leadership style can create serious problems for senior women in terms of how their roles, practices and relationships with others are enacted, received and represented. However, a female leader's language is also strongly shaped by the contexts and communities of practice in which she works. Depending on this context, the gendered nature of leadership language may become a 'problem' for senior women, or alternatively be celebrated as a valuable and distinctive 'asset'.

In order to conclude whether language is indeed a reason why female leaders continue to be under-represented at Boardroom level, I want to give an overview of the multiple insights that have emerged in this book by:

- Reviewing the broader discursive context within which a senior woman's language is enacted, received and represented.
- Defining the language of female leadership as it is shaped by, and interacts with three corporate contexts: Male-Dominated, Gender-Divided and Gender-Multiple.
- Wrapping up: summarising how effective linguistic practices can help to address the continuing problem of the under-representation of senior women in the business world.

Review of the broader discursive context

> Women are at the forefront of Britain's enterprise culture, run-
> ning businesses in areas of heavy industry that have traditionally
> been dominated by men, as well as in social-oriented sectors
> and high-profile areas such as food, fashion, retailing and the
> media.
>
> (Dunne 2009)

We are living in a time of competing discourses about female
leadership. One particularly prevalent discourse appears to be
that of *female success*: the notion of ordinary business women
who achieve extraordinary results. If we read the Business
sections of many quality newspapers in the UK, we may get a
strong impression of female leadership success. For example, a
report on Britain's 100 Most Entrepreneurial Women List
(Dunne 2009) celebrates female leadership and entrepreneurship in both new and established areas such as technology,
forensic science, engineering and manufacturing, not as a competitive rank order but as a group of 'firsts among equals'.
Also frequently profiled in the UK business press are features
about 'celebrity' business women such as Barbara Cassani,
Deborah Meaden, Anne Mulcahy, Nicola Horlick and Nicole Farhi,
who are feted for their exceptional achievements in columns
otherwise filled with more mundane stories about men in grey
suits.

Stories of female success in the media often invoke a theory
of 'gender difference' by implying that women have special if
not *superior* qualities contributing to their success, which clearly
distinguish them from men. This is touched on by Clare Logie,
Head of Women in Business with Bank of Scotland Corporate, when
she explains her view of the reasons for women's success in
entrepreneurship:

> Women are passionate and driven about adding value as
> opposed to purely making a lot of money. We found that
> money is not the key driver for most female entre-
> preneurs. Indeed some women don't even like the tag 'entre-
> preneur'. They just started doing something because they

had an idea and they don't want to be labelled because of that.

(Quoted in Dunne 2009)

Such discursive representations of business women as 'success stories' resulting from their distinctive feminine attributes, is challenged elsewhere by a competing discourse of *gender neutrality*. This is the view that the minority status of women executives does *not* noticeably disadvantage them at senior level (Anderson, Vinnicombe and Singh 2008; Chase 1988; Kanter 1977). Indeed the competing discourses of 'female success' and 'gender neutrality' may be happily espoused by the *same* individual, apparently without too much contradiction. This was the case with Chief Executive Officer of Xerox, Anne Mulcahy who said:

I care a lot about the advancement of women in business and hopefully I can be a champion and a role model...

I try not to do a lot of things that focus on my role as a woman executive. I'm much more focussed on my role as chief executive of Xerox. That's what's meaningful.

(Quoted in Rushe 2002)

According to the gender neutrality discourse, professional women do not wish to be singled out as female. They want their work and achievements to be respected in their own right. However, in order to provide this evidence of gender neutrality, such women often have to work exceptionally hard and perhaps distance themselves from overt sorority with other women. In Chase's terms (1988), this distancing from other women results in a 'gender-blindness' that is appropriated by Male-Dominated corporations that are keen to represent themselves as 'gender-neutral' and as a meritocracy. This was recently exemplified in the research of Kelan and Dunkley Jones (2007), who found evidence of a denial of gender discrimination when interviewing both male and female MBA students, with both women and men downplaying the importance of gender as a factor in career success. These women were concerned *not* to identify too strongly with female support groups such as the UK Women in Business group (Kelan and Dunkley Jones 2007) wishing to preserve a low profile and to be seen as 'ordinary students' who were in no way disadvantaged by their gender. In interpreting these findings, Anderson, Vinnicombe and Singh (2008) suggest that women actually *collude* in conforming to the *status quo*, exhibiting 'gender blindness' to their own experiences of gender discrimination.

In addition to the two discourses of *female success* and *gender neutrality*, a third, competing discourse is that of *female disadvantage* – a representation of women executives which is particularly pervasive in official reports. For example, in the UK government commissioned index on 'Sex and Power' (EOC 2007), the report queried the number of 'missing women' in business, politics, media and the public and voluntary sectors. This estimated that nearly 6,000 women were 'missing' from more than 33,000 positions considered to have power and influence in the UK, which included Members of Parliament, executive and non-executive directors in top multinational companies, public appointments, university vice chancellors, and trades union general secretaries. In this report, the EOC (2007) calculated that at the current rate it would take another 60 years to gain equality of female directors in FTSE 100 companies. This discourse of *female disadvantage* is perhaps the most persuasive discourse of the three, not just because it is initiated by powerful, government-funded agencies, but also because it draws upon a secondary discourse of *scientific rationality* (Litosseliti 2006) to substantiate the shortfall of women in key roles by drawing upon statistical evidence for persuasive effect.

What do we make of these different representations of female leadership in media and institutional discourses? Are women leaders successful or disadvantaged? Can one be regarded as more 'accurate' than the others, a more truthful descriptor of popular attitudes to female leaders?

Certainly, language and gender guru, Deborah Cameron (2003) questions the 'gender difference' assumptions of the *female success* discourse. She argues that this discourse may be 'intended to distract attention from factual evidence suggesting that in material reality women are still "the second sex"' (Cameron 2003: 457). Apparently supporting a discourse of *female disadvantage*, she posits that representations of gender which stress *differences* 'are part of society's apparatus for maintaining gender distinctions in general...in many cases they also help to naturalise gender hierarchies' (Cameron

2003: 452). While Cameron has a point, her perspective here suggests a somewhat dated 'conspiracy theory' view of the world, in which a patriarchal establishment perpetuates its hegemony through society's use of the occasional tokenistic gesture towards women: in this case, publishing media stories focusing on successful women.

So in short, criticisms can be made of the 'accuracy' or 'truthfulness' of any one of these dominant discourses on female leadership. In contrast to attempting to verify the accuracy of *one* specific perspective, I suggest that it is better to understand this 'discursive backdrop' as comprising a ceaseless interaction between *multiple* discourses on female leadership. We have seen in this book that organisations today are pervaded by diverse gendered discourses, so it is quite possible for the discourses of *female success, gender neutrality,* and *female disadvantage* to co-exist without too much sense of contradiction. Thus, internally, organisations are characterised by 'discoursal diversity' (Sunderland 2004: 193), in which varied and interwoven discourses shape different aspects of people's identities. Individuals shift between different subject positions according to contextual and cultural factors: who they are with, the purpose of the engagement, the norms and values of the local community of practice, and so on (Baxter 2003). Each context may have subtly varying expectations and requirements of a person's gendered identity.

Against this backdrop of discoursal diversity, we will see that definitions of the language of female leaders vary considerably according to the type of corporation to which they belong.

The language of female leadership

Is there a language of leadership that is exclusive to women with specific features and characteristics?

The answer is definitely 'yes', but not in the simple sense that there is a distinctive 'woman's language' contrasting with men's, with its own essential and unique qualities and characteristics. This will be disappointing news to those who like to feel that women have something special and different to offer the business world. My own research and that of others in the field (e.g. Marra, Schnurr and Holmes 2006; Mullany 2007) have very clearly shown that both male and female leaders 'do leadership' in very similar ways: they skilfully integrate transactional and relational goals according to contextual factors. *Both* are able to draw upon styles of leadership interaction conventionally coded 'masculine' or 'feminine', and make expedient and skilful use of these.

Despite this finding, there *is* something distinctive that we can call the 'language of female leadership', but perhaps, it is transitional and context-bound. According to my research, female leaders use a style of language that is a more proscribed and self-regulated version of men's, because they need to use special linguistic strategies in order to pre-empt negative evaluation in a business world that continues to be male-dominated (EOC 2007; EHRC 2008). Yet in many ways this style of language is also a highly skilled, linguistically expert, diverse and nuanced version, finely-tuned to colleagues and context.

To what extent do these apparently distinctive aspects of the language of female leadership vary or differ when they interact with different types of corporation? Let's first consider the Male-Dominated corporation.

The Male-Dominated corporation

This type of corporation bears the features described in Kanter's (1977) study of the archetypal business organisation where males as the majority group dominate and marginalise the female minority, supported by structures to sustain the majority's power. Kanter's concepts of 'homophily' and 'tokenism' were based on the idea that people prefer to work with 'similar others'. Through processes of 'assimilation' where stereotyping of women and ethnic minorities is adopted through polarisation of the sexes and exaggeration of their supposed qualities, the boundaries between social groups are heightened. This leads to a strongly male culture, where women are both highly visible yet isolated, and have to work hard to sustain their position. In such contexts, women are positioned and represented by others according to a range of limited and recognised stereotypes (the mother, the seductress, the iron maiden, the pet, etc), which limits their capacity to play an equally recognised and respected role alongside men. While it is obvious to observers that a discourse of *female disadvantage* shapes leadership interactions in this context, it would probably not be recognised as a source of influence by either males or females within the Male-Dominated corporation.

In fact, as we have seen, rather than accepting that they are *victims* of a male-dominated culture, senior women often over-compensate by *neutralising* their gender identity – by *proving* themselves as leaders on the basis of hard work and performance. In order to resist assimilation into one of the gendered stereotypes, senior women are obliged to *regulate* their language by developing a range of 'preemptive strategies' so that they neither appear too assertive and conventionally masculine, nor too tentative and conventionally feminine: in short, they operate the female 'double-bind' (Lakoff 1975). The language of female leadership is therefore principally defined by linguistic regulation, as reported in Chapter 5. However, the expertise that senior women must acquire to monitor and adjust their language in order 'to hit the right professional note' can often be extremely hard work, and ultimately demoralising (Baxter 2008).

Furthermore, there is likely to be a paucity of effective female *role models* for aspiring women to emulate in the Male-Dominated corporation. Ely (1994: 203) found that in firms with few female leaders, women were 'less likely to perceive senior women as role models with legitimate authority, more likely to perceive competition in relationships with women peers'. This of course leads to an atmosphere of suspicion and distrust between women, where conversations 'behind each other's backs' are more likely to occur, and mutual female support is rarely provided in public settings.

In summary, the language of female leaders in the Male-Dominated corporation is one which tends to be highly self-controlled, draws on a range of pre-emptive strategies to resist negative evaluation, and therefore requires considerable effort and energy to achieve. It aims to be 'gender-neutral': neither too masculinised nor feminised in the stereotypical sense. It will be characterised by 'double-voiced discourse' (Chapter 5), that is, highly responsive to audience, context and purpose. However, this responsiveness does not necessarily extend to supporting and defending the interests of other women in the corporation.

How does the definition of the language of female leadership differ when it is shaped by, and interacts with the Gender-Divided corporation?

The Gender-Divided corporation

On the surface, this type of corporation seems a much better prospect for women because it has led to a discourse of *female success*, which proposes that women be allowed to build on their different strengths in order to enhance their position at senior levels.

According to this 'gender difference' view, women leaders make alternative choices to men with regard to their business roles and how they enact them. They also have contrasting needs and expectations of their relationships with colleagues and in relation to getting work done. Ruderman and Ohlott (2004) illustrate this view by suggesting that organisations need to provide support for female leaders in five areas:

- Allow women to act authentically, aligning behaviours needed on a daily basis with their value systems
- Encourage women to make connections, building networks, developing relationships
- Authorise women to act powerfully, rewarding them at the same level as men and allowing them to manage their own careers
- Foster feelings of wholeness, establishing clear priorities and setting boundaries in their work lives
- Enable women to gain self-understanding, providing them with feedback and recognition.

Ruderman and Ohlott (2004: 41–47)

Underlying this somewhat naive perspective is the philosophically essentialist assumption that because women are different from men, they need to connect and engage with others, and have their expressive natures supported by gestures of recognition, approval and feedback. It has led, for example, to the phenomenon of 'women only' leadership courses that, by report, have proved very successful (e.g. Andersen, Vinnicombe and Singh 2008). Such courses place a strong emphasis on the values of 'authenticity' and 'being true to oneself'. However, once again the implication is that women have to put in extra work to set up these special networks, go on these extra courses, and spend time making the case to colleagues that their distinctive viewpoints and approaches are worth adopting within their organisations. The hard work can certainly be worth it. These strategies to support the discourse of *female success* have enormous appeal, because they offer women affirming support structures to help them survive and thrive in organisations that otherwise might marginalise them.

In the Gender-Divided context, the language of female leadership can be defined as one which is characterised by stereotypically feminine attributes: supportive, facilitative, engaged and co-operative. At best, female leaders in this type of corporation could exploit their supposed 'relational' strengths and use these for energising and inspiring colleagues to develop significant organisational changes that would benefit both women and men (Rosener 1990). But what if certain female leaders don't fit into the warm, caring, relational stereotype, and actually have a much more varied or assertive interactional style? At worst, there are likely to be clear expectations from colleagues to speak and behave in certain ways and not in others, which may limit the roles senior women are invited to perform, and the contributions to the organisation they are permitted to make.

So finally, how does the language of female leadership vary or differ when it interacts with, and is shaped by the Gender-Multiple corporation?

The Gender-Multiple corporation

This type of corporation tends *not* to be influenced by the three popular discourses on female leadership reviewed earlier, although there may be traces of all three. The Gender-Multiple corporation doesn't overtly value a discourse of *female success* in the way that the Gender-Divided corporation does, because it would be viewed as fostering a tokenistic or compensatory view of women. Also, the Gender-Multiple corporation doesn't value the discourse of *gender neutrality* because it alternatively recognises the specific contribution of gender alongside other features to be important in shaping people's working lives. Finally, this type of corporation has already assimilated the discourse of *female disadvantage* in its constitutional 'make-up': it actively practises strategies that overturn such disadvantage with policies on promotion, childcare, work-life balance, linguistic expertise, and so on. As a consequence, senior women in the Gender-Multiple corporation have the best opportunity to reach the top of their organisations and once there, to establish their authority and influence. Within this context, a rather different language of leadership is therefore able to flourish, so what defines and characterises it?

Building on emerging practice from key research studies (see Chapter 7), the language of female leadership in the Gender-Multiple corporation can be summarised as being able to:

- Judge how to make skilful use of a repertoire of transactional and relational linguistic strategies to achieve varied business goals according to context and community of practice.

- Support and help to advance more junior female colleagues in public settings.
- Recognise, name, challenge and overturn 'negative' gendered discourses in the corporation.
- Use 'double-voiced' discourse as part of a leader's linguistic expertise or skills-set (rather than used defensively as a strategy to pre-empt criticism).
- Employ a linguistic strategy which uses a judicious blend of 'doing' authority, politeness and humour.
- Benefit from a corporate strategy that challenges negative evaluations of women constructed through sexist language, inappropriate terms to describe women, masculinised metaphors, gendered generalisations, gossip and 'mean talk'.

In order to complete the mission of this book, it is time to summarise how effective linguistic practice can help to address the continuing problem of the under-representation of women at senior level in the business world.

Effective linguistic practices for female leaders

This book has looked at the extraordinary role of *language* in enabling women executives to be effective and powerful leaders in the business world. It has shown how the language we use in our everyday interactions with colleagues is fundamental to constructing and enacting effective leadership identities, roles, relationships, practices and even corporate cultures. On a less positive note, language may also have played a part in contributing to the continuing minority status of senior women in the business world.

So, is language a reason why female leaders continue to be under-represented at senior level?' I believe the answer is 'yes', but that times are changing. In this book, I have proposed two major reasons why female leaders may be disadvantaged by the language they use at senior level. The *first* is that many senior women still work in corporations that are governed by traditional masculine norms. As we saw in Chapter 5, this may place clear restrictions on the ways in which they are permitted or encouraged to speak. In order to avoid being stereotyped, senior women may be compelled to use the self-regulating strategy of 'double-voiced' discourse (Bakhtin 1927/ 1981), so that they sound neither too masculinised nor too feminised. The stamina required to keep up this level of linguistic work may prove too arduous or undermining for some (Baxter 2008). The *second* reason why many senior women continue to be disadvantaged by the language they speak is that they are positioned by gendered discourses that circulate within organisations. Depending on the type of corporation, women will accept or resist discriminatory discourses of *image and sexuality, female emotionality,* or *masculinisation* (as we saw in Chapter 6). However, in the Gender-Multiple corporation, alternative discourses such as *gender equality, diversity* or *gender success* are institutionally approved, and this strengthens women's ability to contest reactionary discourses. As corporations evolve, this could be the future for *all* senior women eventually.

To conclude, I have proposed that effective linguistic practices can help senior women to improve their position in the business world. On an *individual* level, I suggest that they become 'linguistic experts', serving as role models for junior female colleagues. By learning to become 'linguistic role models', women will establish their position in the corporation as leaders of excellence, and contribute to the stock of women that more junior female colleagues look up to and admire. Linguistic expertise can be achieved through a finely modulated use of three forms of language: enacting authority, humour and politeness – in their 'warm' and 'cold' versions. The key here is for a speaker to discriminate within an instant which combination and 'weighting' of strategies is most appropriate for their audience, context and purpose. The case study of Jan, in Chapter 6, gave examples of when this managing director got it absolutely right...and when she occasionally got it wrong.

On a *corporate* level, much more could be done to support senior women in their quest to be linguistic role models within their organisations. The extent to which a corporation takes up such a quest will partly depend on whether it tends towards a Male-Dominated, Gender-Divided or Gender-Multiple corporation. In addition to standard diversity policies, corporations should seek to encourage a greater awareness of how negative attitudes against women are linguistically constructed, which should avoid being presented as 'thought-policing'. In Chapter 7, I proposed the idea of informally appointed 'linguistic champions', some of whom may be senior women, but others of whom might be more junior staff...and male! These champions might play a part in raising awareness, lightly and humorously where possible of such features as people's use of sexist language, terms to describe males and females, metaphor, generalisations and conversations where people 'gossip' about others.

To develop this idea further still, such a linguistic awareness could be accomplished both formally and informally. *Formally,* corporate affairs staff might be trained so that they can apply their linguistic awareness to speech-writing for leaders, in-house publications, as well as to external publications such as recruitment, marketing and publicity materials. There is also a place for dedicated leadership training programmes that include sessions on the use of inclusive language in the organisation.

Informally, linguistic champions can take a role in workshops by pointing out the *options* in language use, indicating how different and alternative ways of describing and evaluating people can have surprisingly different effects. So that, instead of describing a woman leader as 'hard' or 'bossy', she is described as 'strong', 'bold', or 'challenging'. Of course, these alternative words, when applied to a woman, can take on further negative connotations, and this phenomenon in itself is worthy of discussion. A further way of achieving linguistic awareness is by means of a leader's Annual Performance Review. A couple of the objectives set might pertain to linguistic awareness and expertise, both for men and for women. Senior people might be asked on each occasion to assess to what extent they have achieved these linguistic objectives, such as 'range of linguistic strategies used to lead a senior management meeting', or 'ways of inviting junior colleagues to speak in your meetings' or 'ways of describing a colleague of the opposite sex'. The implementation of such formal and informal strategies would no doubt also contribute to a company's reputation as a Gender-Multiple corporation.

Further research needs to be conducted in order to offer female and male leaders a comprehensive template of recognised strategies that might be used to accomplish the language of leadership effectively. But, for this author, that is currently work-in-progress, and will be the subject of another book!

Appendices

Appendix 1   Transcription Conventions (Jefferson 2004)

(.)	Micropause
(1.5)	Pause in tenths of a second
[ ]	Start/finish of overlapping speech or interruption
=	Latching
_	Emphasis
(*Sighs*)	Non-verbal behaviour; editorial comment
?	Rising or questioning intonation
[xxx]	Indecipherable
(ha)	Syllable of laughter
::	Drawing out of the word/syllable

Note: Punctuation is not used to indicate sentence, clause or word boundaries as in conventional written discourse.

Appendix 2   Linguistic Features of Leadership

- Speculating, hypothesising, questioning
- Consulting; seeking help and advice from others
- Establishing status, position in the organisation, expertise, who you know
- Being confrontational, e.g. confronting a person who is being difficult
- Listening
- Dialogue and debate
- Self-promotion: reminding/informing others of your experience, achievements, contacts etc
- Being assertive: making assertions, holding to your opinion
- Being polite and courteous
- Rapport building: aiming to connect, engage, find common ground, empathise
- Extolling a vision
- Being able to give orders and instructions appropriately
- Networking/making and keeping contacts
- Expressing support and solidarity with other people, their views and actions
- Giving praise: complimenting people
- Using humour: witticisms, irony, sarcasm, wry comments, 'taking the mick', jokes
- Being open: expressing uncertainty, admitting mistakes, problems, weaknesses; expressing feelings
- Arguing and developing a case
- Persuading others to your point of view
- Being able to give a speech, presentation or an extended talk in public
- Telling stories and anecdotes

Appendix 3   The Language of Corporate Culture

A	B
• Strong leadership	Open-mindedness
• Propulsion/drive	Engagement
• Growth	Corporate responsibility
• Acquisition	Trust
• Delivery	Commitment
• Performance	Diversity
• Building market shares	Smooth relationships
• Strong balance sheets	Listening and responding
• Strong controls	Communicating with people
• Strong cash flow	Connection
• Tough standards	Treating people as equals

Goal-orientated, competitive, issues of power and control

People-orientated, co-operative, building relationships of empathy and trust

References

Anderson, D., Vinnicombe, S. and Singh, V. (2008) 'Women Only Leadership Development: A Conundrum', in Turnbull James, K. and Collins, J. (eds) *Leadership Learning*, pp. 147–160 (Basingstoke: Palgrave).

Austin, J.J. (1962) *How to Do Things with Words* (Oxford: Clarendon Press).

Bakhtin, M. (1929/1981) *The Dialogic Imagination: Four Essays* (Texas: University of Texas).

Bales, R.F. (1951) *Interaction Process Analysis* (Cambridge MA: Addison-Wesley).

Bales, R.F. (1958) 'Task Roles and Social Roles in Problem-solving Groups', in Macoby, E.E., Newcomb, T.M. and Hartley, E.L. (eds) *Readings in Social Psychology* (New York: Winston).

Bargiela-Chiappini, F. and Harris, S. (1997) *Managing Language: The Discourse of Corporate Meetings* (Amsterdam and Philadelphia: John Benjamins).

Barrett, M. and Davidson, M.J. (eds) (2006) *Gender and Communication at Work* (Aldershot: Ashgate).

Bass, B.M. (1985) *Leadership and Performance Beyond Expectation* (New York: Free Press).

Bass, B.M. and Avolio, B.J. (1993) 'Transformational Leadership: A Response to Critiques', in Chemers, M. and Ayman, R. (eds) *Leadership Theory and Research: Perspectives and Directions*, pp. 49–80 (San Diego, CA: Academic Press).

Baxter, J. (1999) 'Teaching Girls to Speak Out: The Female Voice in Public Contexts', *Language and Education*, 13 (2), 81–98.

—— (2003) *Positioning Gender in Discourse: A Feminist Methodology* (Basingstoke: Palgrave).

—— (2006a) 'Putting Gender in its Place: A Case Study on Constructing Speaker Identities in a Management Meeting', in Barrett, M. and Davidson, M. (eds) *Gender and Communication at Work*, pp. 69–79 (Aldershot: Ashgate Publishing).

—— (ed.) (2006b) *Speaking Out: The Female Voice in Public Contexts* (Basingstoke: Palgrave).

—— (2006c) 'Do We Have to Agree with Her?: How High School Girls Negotiate Leadership in Public Contexts', in Baxter, J. (ed.), pp. 159–178 (Basingstoke: Palgrave).

—— (2008) 'Is it all Tough Talking at the Top?: A Post-structuralist Analysis of the Construction of Gendered Speaker Identities of British Business Leaders within Interview Narratives', *Gender and Language*, 2 (2), 197–222.

—— (2009) 'Outside In-group and Out-group Identities?: Constructing Male Solidarity and Female Exclusion in UK Builders' Talk', *Discourse & Society*, 20 (2), 411–429.

BBC2 (2009) *The Lost Art of Oratory* (London: the British Broadcasting Corporation), 5th May 2009.

Belenky, M.F., Clinchy, B.M., Goldberger, N.R. and Tarule, J.M. (1997) *Women's Ways of Knowing: The Development of Self, Voice and Mind. Tenth anniversary edition* (New York: Basic Books).

Bergvall, V., Bing, J.M. and Freed, A.F. (1996) *Rethinking Language and Gender Research* (London: Longman).

Brewis, J. (2001) 'Telling It Like It Is?: Gender, Language and Organizational Theory', in Westwood, R. and Linstead, S. (eds) *The Language of Organization*, pp. 283–309 (London: Sage).

Brown, P. and Levinson, S. (1987) *Politeness: Some Universals in Language Usage* (Cambridge: Cambridge University Press).

Bucholz, M. and Hall, K. (eds) (1995) *Gender Articulated: Language and the Socially Constructed Self* (New York: Routledge).

Burns, J.M. (1978) *Leadership* (New York: Harper and Rowe).

Butler, J. (1990) *Gender Trouble: Feminism and the Subversion of Identity* (New York: Routledge).

Cameron, D. (1992) *Feminism and Linguistic Theory*, 2nd edn (Basingstoke: Macmillan).

Cameron, D. (1995) *Verbal Hygiene* (London: Routledge).

Cameron, D. (1996) 'The Language-gender Interface: Challenging Co-optation', in Bergvall, V.L., Bing, J.M. and Freed, A.F. (eds) *Rethinking Language and Gender Research: Theory and Practice*, pp. 31–53 (London: Longman).

Cameron, D. (1997) 'Performing Gender Identity: Young Men's Talk and the Construction of Heterosexual Masculinity', in Johnson, S. and Meinhof, U. (eds) *Language and Masculinity*, pp. 47–64 (Oxford: Blackwell).

Cameron, D. (2001) *Working with Spoken Discourse* (London: Sage).

Cameron, D. (2003) 'Gender and Language Ideologies', in Holmes, J. and Meyerhoff, M. (eds) *Handbook of Gender and Language Research*, pp. 447–467 (Oxford: Basil Blackwell).

Cameron, D. (2006) 'Theorising the Female Voice in Public Contexts', in Baxter, J. (ed.), pp. 3–20 (Basingstoke: Palgrave).

Cameron, D. (2007) *The Myth of Mars and Venus* (Oxford: Oxford University Press).

Cameron, D. and Kulick, D. (2003) *Language and Sexuality* (Cambridge: Cambridge University Press).

Campbell, M. and Watt, H. (2007) 'Wonder Woman or Traitor to her Sex?', *The Sunday Times*, p. 14 (London: The Sunday Times).

Catalyst and Opportunity Now (2000) *Breaking the Barriers: Women in Senior Management in the UK* (London: Business in the Community).

Chase, S.E. (1988) 'Making Sense of the Woman Who Becomes a Man', in Todd, A.D. and Fisher, S. (eds) *Gender and Discourse: The Power of Talk*, pp. 275–295 (Norwood, New Jersey: Ablex).

Coates, J. (1995) 'Language, Gender and Career', in Mills, S. (ed.) *Language and Gender: Interdisciplinary Perspectives*, pp. 135–148 (London: Longman).

Coates, J. (1996) *Women Talk* (Oxford: Blackwell).

Coates, J. (2004) *Women, Men and Language*, 2nd edn (London: Longman).

Connell, R.W. (1995) *Masculinities* (Berkeley: California: University of California Press).

Consalvo, C.M. (1989) 'Humor in Management: No Laughing Matter', *Humor*, 2 (3), 285–297.

Cooper, R. (1989) 'Modernism, Post-modernism and Organisational Analysis 3: The Contribution of Jacques Derrida', *Organisation Studies*, 10 (4), 479–502.

Crawford, M. (1995) *Talking Difference: On Gender and Language* (London: Sage).

Davidson, M.J. and Burke, R.J. (eds) (1994) *Women in Management: Current Research Issues* (London: Paul Chapman).

DeFrancisco, V. (1991) 'The Sounds of Silence: How Men Silence Women in Marital Relations', *Discourse & Society*, 2 (4), 413–423.

De Katdt, E. (2002) 'An Introduction to "Gender and Language"', *Southern African Linguistics and Applied Language Studies*, 20 (3), iii–v.

Decker, W. and Rotondo, D. (2001) 'Relationships among Gender, Type of Humour and Perceived Leadership Effectiveness', *Journal of Managerial Issues*, 13 (4), 451–465.

Derrida, J. (1987) *A Derrida Reader: Between the Blinds* (Brighton: Harvester Press).

Dunne, H. (2009) 'There are 100 Reasons to Celebrate', *The Daily Telegraph*, 4.3.09, p. B8 (London: The Telegraph Newspapers).

Eagly, A. and Johnson, B. (1990) 'Gender and Leadership Style: A Meta-analysis', *Psychological Bulletin*, 108 (2), 233–256.

Eagly, A. and Carli, L. (2007) *Through the Labyrinth: The Truth about how Women become Leaders* (Boston: Harvard Business School Press).

Eckert, P. (2000) *Linguistic Variation as Social Practice* (Oxford: Blackwell).

Eckert, P. and McConnell-Ginet, S. (1998) 'Communities of Practice: Where Language, Gender and Power All Live', in Coates, J. (ed.) *Language and Gender: A Reader*, pp. 484–494 (Oxford: Blackwell).

EHRC (2008) *Sex and Power 2008* (London: Equality and Human Rights Commission).

Ely, R. (1994) 'The Effects of Organisational Demographics and Social Identity among Professional Women', *Administrative Science Quarterly*, 39, 203–238.

EOC (2007) *Sex and Power: Who Runs Britain?* (London: The Equal Opportunities Commission).

Eskilson, A. and Wiley, M.G. (1976) 'Sex Composition and Leadership in Small Groups', *Sociometry*, 39, 183–194.

Fishman, P. (1978) 'Interaction: The Work Women Do', *Social Problems*, 25 (4), 397–406.

Fletcher, J.K. (1999) *Disappearing Acts: Gender, Power and Relational Practice at Work* (Cambridge, MA: MIT Press).

Foucault, M. (1972) *The Archeology of Knowledge and the Discourse on Language* (New York: Pantheon).

Foucault, M. (1980) *Power/Knowledge* (Brighton: Harvester Press).

Freed, A. (1996) 'Language and Gender Research in an Experimental Setting', in Bergvall, V.L., Bing, J.M. and Freed, A.F. (eds), pp. 54–76 (London: Longman).

Gibson, D.E. (2004) 'Role Models in Career Development: New Directions for Theory and Research', *Journal of Vocational Behaviour*, 65, 134–156.

Gilligan, C. (1989) *Mapping the Moral Domain: A Contribution of Women's Thinking to Psychological Theory and Education* (Cambridge, Massachusetts: Harvard University Press).

Gold, R.L. (1958) 'Roles in Sociological Fieldwork', *Social Forces*, 36, 217–223.

Goodwin, M.H. (1998) 'Cooperation and Competition across Girls' and Boys' Play Activities', in Coates, J. (ed.) *Language and Gender: A Reader*, pp. 121–146 (Blackwell: Oxford).

Gray, J. (1992) *Men are from Mars and Women from Venus* (New York: Harper-Collins).

Gray. J. (2002) *Mars and Venus in the Workplace: A Practical Guide for Improving Communication and Getting Results at Work* (London and New York: Harper-Collins).

Grint, K. (1997) *Leadership, Classical, Contemporary and Critical Approaches* (Oxford: Oxford University Press).

Gutek, B. and Morasch, B. (1982) 'Sex Ratios, Sex-role Spill-over and Sexual Harassment of Women at Work', *Journal of Social Issues*, 38, 58–74.

Halford, S. and Leonard, P. (2001) *Gender, Power and Organisations* (Basingstoke: Palgrave).

Hammersley, M. and Atkinson, P. (1995) *Ethnography: Principles in Practice*, 2nd edn (London: Routledge).

Harrington, K., Litosseliti, L., Saunston, H. and Sunderland, J. (eds) (2008) *Gender and Language Research Methodologies* (Basingstoke: Palgrave).

Hayward, S. (2005) *Women Leading* (Basingstoke: Palgrave).

Heath, A., Steiner, R., Cave, A. and Boyle, C. (2007) 'Anatomy of British Business', *The Business*, 6 January 2007, pp. 22–24.

Heilbrunn, J. (1989) 'Make Love, Not War', *Marketing News*, 30 January, pp. 4, 18.

Helgesen, S. (1990) *The Female Advantage: Women's Ways of Leadership* (New York: Doubleday/Currency).

Hochschild, A. (1974) 'Making It: Marginality and Obstacles to Minority Consciousness', in Kundsin, R. (ed.) *Women and Success*, pp. 66–78 (New York: William Morrow and Co, Inc).

Holmes, J. (1992) 'Women's Talk in Public Contexts', *Discourse and Society*, 3 (2), 131–150.

Holmes, J. (1995) *Women, Men and Politeness* (London: Longman).

Holmes, J. (2000) 'Women at Work: Analysing Women's Talk in New Zealand Workplaces', *Australian Review of Applied Linguistics (ARAL)*, 22 (2), 1–17.

Holmes, J. (2001) *An Introduction to Sociolinguistics*, 2nd edn (London: Longman).

Holmes, J. (2006) *Gendered Talk at Work* (Oxford: Blackwell).

Holmes, J. and Marra, M. (2004) 'Relational Practice in the Workplace: Women's Talk or Gendered Discourse?', *Language in Society*, 33, 377–398.

Holmes, J. and Stubbe, M. (2003) *Power and Politeness in the Workplace. A Sociolinguistic Analysis of Talk at Work* (London: Longman).

Jefferson, G. (2004) 'Glossary of Transcript Symbols with an Introduction', in Lerner, G.H. (ed.) *Conversation Analysis: Studies from the First Generation*, pp. 13–23 (Philadelphia: John Benjamins).

Jesperson, O. (1922) *Language, its Nature, Development and Origin* (London: George Allen and Unwin).

Johnson, S. (2009) 'EU Bans "Sexist" Use of Miss and Mrs', *The Daily Telegraph*, 16.3.09, p. 1 (London: The Telegraph Newspapers).

Jones, D. (1980) 'Gossip: Notes on Women's Oral Culture', in Cameron, D. (ed.) *The Feminist Critique of Language*, pp. 242–250 (London: Routledge).

Jule, A. (2006) 'Silence as Morality: Lecturing at a Theological College', in Baxter, J. (ed.), pp. 103–120 (Basingstoke: Palgrave).

Kanter, R.M. (1977) *Men and Women of the Corporation* (New York: Basic Books).

Katz, B. (1989) *Turning Practical Communication into Business Power* (London: Mercury).

Kelan, E.K. and Dunkley Jones, R. (2007) 'Gender in the MBA', *Working Paper 1* (London Business School: The Lehman Brothers Centre for Women in Business).

Kendall, S. (2006) 'Positioning the Female Voice within Work and Family', in Baxter, J. (ed.), pp. 179–197 (Basingstoke: Palgrave).

Kimura, D. (1999) *Sex and Cognition* (Cambridge, MA: MIT Press).

Koller, V. (2004) *Metaphor and Gender in Business Media Discourse* (Basingstoke: Palgrave).

Korabik, K. (1982) 'Sex-role Orientation and Leadership Style', *International Journal of Women's Studies*, 5, 328–336.

Korabik, K. (1990) 'Androgyny and Leadership Style', *Journal of Business Ethics*, 283–292.

Kotter, J. (2001) 'What Leaders Really Do', *Harvard Business Review. Special Issue on Leadership*, 79 (11), 85–96.

Kress, G. and van Leeuwen, T. (1996) *Reading Images: The Grammar of Visual Design* (London: Routledge).

Lakoff, R. (1975) *Language and Woman's Place* (New York: Harper and Row).

Lakoff, G. and Johnson, M. (1980) *Metaphors We Live By* (Chicago: University of Chicago Press).

Lave, J. and Wenger, E. (1991) *Situated Learning: Legitimate Peripheral Participation* (Cambridge: Cambridge University Press).

Legge, K. (1995) *Human Resource Management: Rhetorics and Realities* (Basingstoke: Macmillan).

Liff, S. and Cameron, I. (1997) 'Changing Equality Cultures to Move beyond "Women's Problems"', *Gender, Work and Organisation*, 4 (1), 35–46.

Litosseliti, L. (2006a) *Gender and Language: Theory and Practice* (London: Hodder & Arnold).

Litosseliti, L. (2006b) 'Constructing Gender in Public Arguments: The Female Voice as Emotional Voice', in Baxter, J. (ed.), pp. 240–260 (Basingstoke: Palgrave).

Lockheed, M.E. and Hall, K.P. (1976) 'Conceptualising Sex as a Status Characteristic: Applications to Leadership Training Strategies', *Journal of Social Issues*, 32, 11–124.

Lyotard, J. (1984) *The Post-modern Condition* (Manchester: Manchester University Press).

Maddock, S. and Parkin, D. (1993) 'Gender Cultures: Women's Choices and Strategies at Work', *Women in Management Review*, 8 (2), 3–9.

Maltz, D. and Borker, R. (1982) 'A Cultural Approach to Male-Female Mis-communication', in J. Gumperz (ed.) *Language and Social Identity*, pp. 196–216 (Cambridge: Cambridge University Press).

Marra, M., Schnurr, S. and Holmes, J. (2006) 'Effective Leadership in New Zealand: Balancing Gender and Role', in Baxter, J. (ed.), pp. 240–260 (Basingstoke: Palgrave).

McCall, J.B. and Cousins, J. (1990) *Communication Problem Solving: The Language of Effective Management* (Chichester: Wiley and Sons).

McConnell-Ginet, S. (2000) 'Breaking through the "Glass Ceiling": Can Linguistic Awareness Help?', in J. Holmes (ed.), *Gendered Speech in Social Context: Perspectives from Gown and Town*, pp. 259–282 (Wellington: Victoria University Press).

Mesthrie, (2000) 'Social Dialectology', in Mesthrie, R., Swann, J., Deumert, A. and Leap, W.L. (eds) *Introducing Sociolinguistics*, pp. 76–112 (Edinburgh: Edinburgh University Press).

Miller, C. and Swift, K. (1981) *The Handbook of Non-Sexist Writing* (London: The Women's Press).

Mills, S. (1997) *Discourse* (London: Routledge).

Mills, S. (2003) 'Third Wave Feminism and the Analysis of Sexism', *Discourse Analysis Online*, refereed interactive e-journal: www.shu.ac.uk/aol.

Mills, S. (2006) 'Gender and Performance Anxiety at Academic Conferences', in Baxter, J. (ed.), pp. 61–80 (Basingstoke: Palgrave).

Morreall, J. (1991) 'Humor and Work', *Humor: International Journal of Humor Research*, 4 (4), 359–373.

Mullany, L. (2007) *Gendered Discourse in Professional Communication* (Basingstoke: Palgrave).

Newton, D. (1979) *Think like a Man, Act like a Lady and Work like a Dog* (New York: Knopf Doubleday Publishing Group).

Olsson, S. (2006) 'We Don't Need Another Hero!: Organisational Story-telling as a Vehicle for Communicating a Female Archetype of Workplace Leadership', in Barrett, M. and Davidson, M.J. (eds), pp. 195–210 (Aldershot: Ashgate).

Olsson, S. and Walker, R. (2003) 'The Wo-men and the Boys: Patterns of Identification and Differentiation in Senior Women Executives Representations of Career Identity', *Proceedings of ANZCA03: Designing Communication for Diversity*, Brisbane, July 2003 www.bgsb.qut.edu.au/conferences/ANZCA03/Proceedings/default.htm.

Paramount Pictures (2004) *Mean Girls* (Los Angeles: Paramount Pictures).

Pauwels, A. (1989) 'Some Thoughts on Gender, Inequality and Language Reform', *Vox*, 3, 78–87.

Peace, W.H. (2001) 'The Hard Work of Being a Soft Manager', *Harvard Business Review*, December 2001, 99–104.

Pease, A. and Pease, B. (2001) *Why Men Don't Listen and Women Can't Read Maps* (London: Orion Press).

Pemberton, C. (1995) 'Organisational Culture and Equalities Work', in Shaw, J. and Perrons, D. (eds) *Making Gender Work: Managing Equal Opportunities* (Buckingham: Open University Press).

Pichler, P. (2008) 'Gender, Ethnicity and Religion in Spontaneous Talk and Ethnographic Interviews: Balancing Perspectives of Researcher and Researched', in Harrington, K., Litosseliti, L., Saunston, H. and Sunderland, J. (eds), pp. 56–70 (Basingstoke: Palgrave).

Petty, M.M. and Miles, R.H. (1976) 'Leader Sex-role Stereotyping in a Female Dominated Work Culture', *Personnel Psychology*, 29, 393–404.

Pinker, S. (2002) *The Blank Slate: The Modern Denial of Human Nature* (London: Allen Lane).

Pinker, S. (2008) *The Sexual Paradox: Troubled Boys, Gifted Girls and the Real Differences between the Sexes* (London: Atlantic Books).

Powell, G.N. (2000) 'The Glass Ceiling: Explaining the Good and the Bad News', in Davidson, M. and Burke, R. (eds) *Women in Management: Current Research Issues. Vol. 2*, pp. 236–249 (London: Sage).

Riley, S., Frith, H., Archer, L. and Veseley, L. (2006) 'Institutional Sexism in Academia', *The Psychologist*, 19 (2), 94–97.

Rojo, R.M. and Esteban, C.G. (2003) 'Discourse at Work: When Women Take on the Role of Manager', in Weiss, G. and Wodak, R. (eds) *Critical Discourse Analysis: Theory and Interdisciplinarity* (Basingstoke: Palgrave).

Rosener, J.B. (1990) 'Ways Women Lead', *Harvard Business Review*, 68, 119–125.

Ruderman, M. and Ohlott, P. (2004) 'What Women Leaders Want', *Leader to Leader*, 31, 41–47.

Rushe, D. (2002) 'Some Blondes Have no Time for Fun', *The Sunday Times*, 20th October 2002, p. 3.7 (London: The Sunday Times Newspapers).

Schein, V.E. (1975) 'Relationships between Sex-role Stereotypes and Requisite Management Characteristics among Female Managers', *Journal of Applied Psychology*, 60, 340–344.

Schnurr, S. (2008) *Leadership Discourse at Work. Interactions of Humour, Gender and Workplace Culture* (Basingstoke: Palgrave).

Schulz, M.R. (1975) 'The Semantic Derogation of Women', in Thorne, B. and Henley, N. (eds) *Language and Sex: Difference and Dominance*, pp. 64–75 (Rowley, Massachusetts: Newbury House).

Sealy, R., Vinnicombe, S. and Singh, V. (2008) *The Female FTSE Index and Report 2008* (London: Cranfield University School of Management).

Sealy, R. and Singh, V. (2008) 'The Importance of Role Models in the Development of Leaders' Professional Identities', in Turnbull James, K. and Collins, J. (eds) *Leadership Perspectives: Knowledge into Action*, pp. 208–222 (Basingstoke: Palgrave).

Searle, J. (1969) *Speech Acts: An Essay in the Philosophy of Language* (Cambridge: Cambridge University Press).

Senge, P. (1994) *The Fifth Discipline* (London: Nicholas Brearley Publishing).

Shamir, B. (1995) 'Social Distance and Charismatic Leadership: Theoretical Notes and an Exploratory Study', *Leadership Quarterly*, 6 (1), 19–47.

Shannon, C. and Weaver, W. (1949) *The Mathematical Theory of Communication* (Illinois: University of Illinois Press).

Shapiro, E., Haseltine, F. and Rowe, M. (1978) 'Moving Up: Role Models, Mentors and the Patron System', *Sloan Management Review*, 19, 51–58.

Shaw, B. (1916) *Pygmalion* (New York: Brentano).

Sheldon, A. (1992) 'Conflict Talk: Sociolinguistic Challenges to Self-assertion and How Young Girls Meet Them', *Merrill-Palmer Quarterly*, 38 (1), 95–117.

Sinclair, A. (1994) 'The Australian Executive Culture: Heroes and Women', in Carroll, P. (ed.) *Feminine Forces: Redefining the Workplace: Women and Leadership National Conference Proceedings*, pp. 180–193 (Perth: Edith Cowan University).

Sinclair, A. (1998) *Doing Leadership Differently. Gender, Power and Sexuality in a Changing Business Culture* (Melbourne: Melbourne University Press).

Singh, V. (2002) 'Diversity: Think Different', *Director*, July 2002, pp. 25–26.

Singh, V. (2007) 'Women Breaking through the Glass Ceiling', *The Effective Executive* (Hyderabad: ICFAI Business School), July 2007 issue.

Singh, V. (2008) *Transforming Boardroom Cultures in Science, Engineering and Technology Organisations* (UKRC for Women in SET: Bradford).

Singh, V., Vinnicombe, S. and James, K. (2006) 'Constructing a Professional Identity: How Young Female Managers Use Role Models', *Women in Management Review*, 21 (1), 67–81.

Spence, J.T., Helmreich, R. and Stapp, J. (1975) 'Ratings of Self and Peers on Sex Role Attributes and their Relation to Self-esteem and Conceptions of Masculinity and Femininity', in *Journal of Personality and Social Psychology*, 32 (1), 29–39.

Spender, D. (1980) *Man Made Language* (London: Pandora).

Still, L. (2006) 'Gender, Leadership and Communication', in Barrett, M. and Davidson, M.J. (eds), pp. 183–191 (Aldershot: Ashgate).

Strodbeck, F. and Mann, R. (1956) 'Sex Role Differentiation in Jury Deliberations', *Sociometry*, 19, 3–11.

Sunderland, J. (2004) *Gendered Discourses* (Basingstoke: Palgrave).

Swann, J. (2002) 'Yes, but Is It Gender?', in Litosseliti, L. and Sunderland, J. (eds) *Gender Identity and Discourse Analysis*, pp. 43–67 (Amsterdam: John Benjamins).

Tajfel, H. (1978) *Differentiation between Social Groups: Studies in the Social Psychology of Inter-group Relations* (London: Academic Press).

Talbot, M. (1998) *Language and Gender: An Introduction* (Oxford: Polity Press).

Tannen, D. (1990) *You Just Don't Understand!* (London: Virago).

Tannen, D. (1994a) *Gender and Discourse* (London: Oxford University Press).

Tannen, D. (1994b) *Talking from 9 to 5: Women and Men in the Workplace: Language and Sex and Power* (New York: Avon).

Terjesen, S. and Singh, V. (2008) 'Female Presence on Corporate Boards: A Multi-Country Study of Environmental Context', *Journal of Business Ethics*, 83, 55–63.

Thomson, P. and Graham, J. (2008) *A Woman's Place is in the Boardroom: The Roadmap* (Basingstoke: Palgrave).

Tracy, K. and Dimmock, A. (2004) 'Meetings: Discursive Sites for Building and Fragmenting Community', in Kalbfleisch, P. (ed.) *Communication Yearbook 28*, pp. 127–166 (Thousand Oaks, CA: Sage).

Trudgill, P. (2000) *Sociolinguistics: An Introduction to Language and Society*, 4th edn (London: Penguin).

Vinicombe, S. and Singh, V. (2002) 'Sex Role Stereotyping and Requisites of Successful Top Managers', *Women in Management Review*, 120–130.

Vinnicombe, S., Singh, V., Burke, R., Bilimoria, D. and Huse, M. (2009) *Women on Corporate Boards of Directors* (London: Edward Elgar).

Walters-York, L.M. (1996) 'Metaphor in Accounting Discourse', *Accounting, Auditing and Accountability Journal*, 9 (5), 45–70.

Watson, J. (2007) 'Accessed Voice as Part of a News Report on the EOC Report', *Sex and Power: Who Runs Britain?* (London: The Equal Opportunities Commission).

Weatherall, A. (2002) *Gender, Language and Discourse* (London: Routledge).

Weber, M. (1947) *The Theory of Social and Economic Organisation*, trans. Henderson, A.M. and Parsons, T. (New York: Free Press).

Weedon, C. (1997) *Feminist Practice and Poststructuralist Theory*, 2nd edn (Oxford: Blackwell).

Wenger, E. (1998) *Communities of Practice* (Cambridge and New York: Cambridge University Press).

West, C. (1984/1998) 'When the Doctor is a "Lady": Power, Status and Gender in Physician-Patient Encounters', in Coates, J. (ed.) *Language and Gender: A Reader*, pp. 396–412 (Oxford: Blackwell).

Wilson, F. (1992) 'Language, Technology, Gender and Power', *Human Relations*, 45 (9), 883–904.

Wodak, R. (1997) 'I Know We Won't Revolutionise the World with This, but ...' Styles of Female Leadership in Institutions', in Kotthoff, H. and Wodak, R. (eds) *Communicating Gender in Context*, pp. 335–370 (Amsterdam: Benjamins).

Index